WITHDRAWN
NDSU

THE THREE WARTONS

A comprehensive and representative selection (amounting to at least half) from their verse, edited by Eric Partridge, with introduction, critical handlists (very much fuller than the modest foreword has led many estimable persons to suppose), and notes. *Demy 8vo ; printed in Baskerville by the Oxford University Press ; 550 copies at 7s. 6d., 150 on Batchelor's Kelmscott paper at 21s.*

> *Times Literary Supplement :* " The bibliography, like the introduction, is valuable."
>
> *Modern Language Notes :* " The rehabilitation of the Wartons may be regarded as complete with the publication of this beautiful book."

BLAKE'S POETICAL SKETCHES

This book was published to obviate the neglect into which the *Poetical Sketches* had fallen in comparison with the no-whit-superior *Songs*, and apparently the aim was justified. There is a general introduction on Blake's lyrics, with especial reference to the *Sketches*, while Jack Lindsay, the poet-critic, has written a long study on Blake's metric—a luminous criticism that is valuable not merely for Blake but for the whole study of English poetry. *Crown 4to ; 14 pt. Garamond ; distinctively printed by the Westminster Press ; 545 numbered copies at 9s. ; 75, signed by Jack Lindsay, at 30s. ; both editions most attractively bound ; very few copies of the fine edition remain.*

> *Times Literary Supplement :* " Excellent essay on Blake's metric."
>
> *Bookman :* " This well-printed and spacious edition is rendered the more attractive and valuable by Mr. Jack Lindsay's vital essay on Blake's metric."

THREE PLAYS

By NICHOLAS ROWE

Edited by J. R. Sutherland, with a life that contains much new information ; with a criticism of Rowe's works that throws new light on eighteenth-century drama both acted and published ; with a critical text, a descriptive bibliography, and notes. *Royal 8vo ; beautifully printed by the Cambridge University Press in Fournier ; 660 copies at 21s. (the price was raised after March 31st, 1929 ; but is still low from the financial point of view) ; 65 bound in buckram at 42s. Selected by the British Museum for their exhibition of fine-press work.*

> *Manchester Guardian*, review by Professor H. B. CHARLTON : " [These plays] are an historical link in the life of English drama, and Mr. Sutherland's edition would be justified by historical necessity if it were not amply warranted by the editor's scholarly way of performing his task."

THE POEMS OF HENRY CAREY

THE POEMS OF HENRY CAREY

Edited by F. T. WOOD

Published by Eric Partridge Ltd.

Printed by John Wright and Sons Ltd., at Bristol, England
In 12 point Imprint on Antique Wove paper.

Bound by Gordon Innes and Co. Ltd.

Limited to 560 copies.
The first five signed by the editor.

THE POEMS OF
HENRY CAREY

EDITED WITH AN INTRODUCTION AND NOTES

BY

FREDERICK T. WOOD

THE SCHOLARTIS PRESS : ERIC PARTRIDGE LTD.

THIRTY MUSEUM STREET, LONDON

821
C18

PR
3339
C23
A17
1930

Lib.

1. 75~

Henneman

3-9-46

PREFACE

IN compiling this volume the object has been to give, as far as possible, a complete edition of the poems of Carey, a project never before undertaken either during the author's lifetime or since his death. All possible sources have been drawn upon, and though it is too much to hope that every extant poem of so elusive a person has been tracked down, every attempt to that end has been made. The bulk of the work consists, naturally, of those pieces contained in the three editions of the *Poems on Several Occasions* and of *The Musical Century*, but several poems and cantatas have been taken from *The Gentleman's Magazine* and other periodicals, as well as from various miscellanies and anthologies. Every piece printed in *The Musical Century*, however, will not be found in the present volume, for though Carey claimed to be the author of " the words and music of the whole " of those collections, in a number of cases he wrote the music only. Where, therefore, there seemed to be sufficient evidence to warrant the assumption that the words were not his, the piece has not been included. For the sake of completeness, on the other hand, several pieces of doubtful authorship, though probably by Carey, have been included, and a note has in each case been added.

As a question so debatable could not have been dealt with adequately in so short a space, any detailed

7

74361

discussion of the authorship of *God Save the King* has been purposely omitted. For that the reader is referred to R. Clark's *The National Anthem* (1822), W. H. Cummings' *God Save the King* (1904), and the numerous other works on the subject.

To have included the songs and lyrics from Carey's dramatic works would have increased the size of the book considerably, and since, after all, they are to be regarded as parts of a larger whole rather than as separate poems, they have been omitted unless there was any special reason for including them.

Carey's poems are not of the type which calls for very detailed annotation, and in writing the notes, therefore, I have endeavoured to make them as few and as concise as possible, but yet such as will satisfy at one and the same time the needs of the scholar and those of the more casual reader of verse.

A few words are perhaps necessary on the spelling and punctuation. In most cases, where no possible ambiguity could result, the original spelling has been retained, but it has been thought advisable to modernize the punctuation. The initial capitals in nouns, in the use of which the eighteenth century was very lavish, have also been dispensed with.

FREDERICK T. WOOD.

Eden House,

   Paddock Wood, Kent.

January 18, 1930.

CONTENTS

9

INTRODUCTION

TO the average student of English literature the name of Henry Carey probably suggests very little. A minor poet, who had the misfortune to live an obscure life in an age which, until recent years, has itself been obscure, was foredoomed to an early literary interment. Happily the tide is now turning, and Augustan literature is coming into its own. The present phenomenal revival of interest in the life and literature of the early eighteenth century unearths to us daily works and authors the very existence of whom was yesterday all but unsuspected. Memoirs and diaries are reprinted, satires, pamphlets and literary squibs are raked out from the scrap-heap of antiquity and graced with long and learned introductions and notes. And this, despite those who would persuade us that the neo-classic age was devoid of any widespread literary excellence, is all to the good. The Gays, the Popes, and the Swifts we have known for long, but neither in art nor in thought, by the very greatness of their genius, can they be taken as typical of the Augustan era. A true realization of the spirit of the age is only to be gained by a close familiarity with that large band of minor, though by no means despicable writers who, quietly and unobtrusively, were shaping the destinies of English literature during those years when Marlborough and Walpole were making English history. All played their little part in the movements of the time, although to-day their names appear only on that long list of forgotten worthies of literature. Perhaps the most completely forgotten of them all is Henry Carey, now remembered only for two works, his ballad of *Sally in Our Alley*, and the burlesque tragedy of *Chrononhotonthologos*, and even for these credit is but grudgingly bestowed upon him. Yet his work is hardly so mediocre as to merit this neglect. In poetry, it is true, he was no Pope, nor was he a Swift, yet he rises as far above mediocrity as do many of his more fortunate fellows who still find a place in text-books of literature. He seems long ago to have sunk into obscurity, but it is perhaps not yet too late to rescue him from total oblivion.

It is a feature of history that it can show a number of mystery personages who from time to time make their appearance as it were from nowhere, pass dimly across the literary horizon, and then vanish. Such is Henry Carey. The date and place of his birth, as well as his parentage, are both a mystery. The details of his life are obscure, though the main incidents are plain enough and can be traced with fair accuracy. Henry Carey was born, in all probability, in the year 1687 or thereabout, for the parish register of St. James' Church, Clerkenwell, where he was buried on October 5, 1743, gives his age at the time of his death as fifty-six. An entry in a church register, of course, is by no means infallible, but it is improbable that if there were an error it would be a great one. He has long been reputed to have been an illegitimate son of the great George Savile, Marquis of Halifax, but though there is little evidence to disprove this report there is but meagre to substantiate it. It seems evident, however, that in some way or other he was connected with the Saviles, for to several of his sons he gave the name of a distinguished member of that house,[1] while practically all his patrons were members or connections of the Savile family.[2] The one document which might have helped to solve the problem, a manuscript *Memoirs of the Life of George Savile*, compiled by himself, was unfortunately destroyed some thirty years after its author's death, and although all of Savile's extant correspondence has been collected by Miss H. C. Foxcroft, and published as *The Life and Letters of George Savile*, these throw no light upon the question. Miss Foxcroft, indeed, repudiates the rumour which has persisted for a hundred and fifty years, and suggests that confusion has arisen with another member of the family, possibly William, the second Marquis.

While agreeing that such a confusion has probably arisen, I would suggest that it is not with the second Marquis, but with Henry, a younger son of George Savile, who later became Lord Eland. An early nineteenth century authority states that Carey was a posthumous child, and therefore, since George Savile died late in the year 1695, places his birth in the early months of 1696. In point of fact, however, we have seen that he was probably born in 1687. Henry Savile was born in February, 1661, and was baptized on March 2, of the same year at the parish church of St. James, Clerkenwell, with which, it may be noted in passing, Carey himself and his whole family were closely connected. He died on October 10, 1687, and Carey, therefore, were he his son, might well have been born posthumously.

---

[1] Henry Savile Carey (b. 28/2/1737), George Savile Carey (b. 11/11/1738) and William Savile Carey (b. 25/2/1740).

[2] Dorothy Countess Burlington, to whom the *Poems on Several Occasions* were dedicated, was the daughter of William Savile. To her husband, Richard Earl of Burlington, Carey dedicated his opera *Teraminta*. Lord Chesterfield, to whom *Of Stage Tyrants* was addressed, was a grandson by marriage of George Savile, while Charles Viscount Bruce, to whom *The Musical Century* was dedicated, was a son-in-law of William Savile.

It seems probable that he was a native of Yorkshire. The Saviles had been a family long established in the West Riding, and this fact alone would tend to connect Carey with the same locality. Many of his plays, too, have their scenes laid in that county. The farce *Hanging and Marriage* (1722), is founded in a small Yorkshire village ; the scene of the burlesque opera *The Dragon of Wantley* is the little village of Wantley, or Wharncliffe, near Sheffield, while the title of *The Honest Yorkshireman* speaks for itself ; and in two of these pieces at least the author displays an intimate knowledge of the Yorkshire dialect such as only a native, or one very familiar with the district, could possess.

The identity of the poet's mother is even more obscure than is that of his father. It has been asserted that she was a young schoolmistress, a supposition somewhat defective in that it is based on the single fact that a poem of Carey's is described by the author as having formed part of " an entertainment given at Mrs. Carey's school."[1] It is evident, however, from a reference in it to the treaty of Utrecht, that this poem was written in 1713, and as Carey would then be about twenty-six years of age the Mrs. Carey referred to may have been, not his mother, but his wife.

His mother's name, indeed, may never have been Carey at all, for it seems probable that in his early life the poet used the surname of his putative father, and that Carey was only adopted later. In the parish register of Rothwell, a village situated near Rotherham in Yorkshire, the scene of the supposed ravages of the Dragon of Wantley, is recorded under the date April 4, 1708, the marriage of a certain Henry Savile and Sarah Dobson. Now a search of the genealogical tables of the Savile family reveals the fact that at this

---

[1] See page 57.

time the only Henry Savile alive in the normal line was never married, and therefore the person whose marriage is here recorded must have been either of another family altogether, or else an illegitimate connection, whose name does not, therefore, appear in the genealogy. The comparative rarity of the name tends to rule out the former assumption, so that one is tempted very strongly to give credence to the alternative, and suppose that this Henry Savile was no other than the person who was later known in the world of letters as Henry Carey. At this time Carey would be about twenty-one years old, an age at which it is quite likely that he would marry. We know, moreover, that the Christian name of his wife was Sarah, for her name is frequently entered as Sarah Carey in the registers of the church of St. James, Clerkenwell, while the same name also appears in the letters of administration which were granted to her over her husband's property after his death. Here, then, in the very midst of the district with which Carey seems to have been intimately connected, we find a person bearing a Christian name identical with that of the poet, and the surname of his putative father, marrying a woman with the same Christian name as his wife. The implication is obvious.

When Carey came to London is not clear, but it must have been before 1713, for in that year he issued his first volume of poems from the capital. It is not unlikely that the changing of his name coincided with this change of environment. To a young man anxious to make his way in the world the stigma of illegitimacy must have appeared a dangerous impediment which he would wish, if possible, to hide, and his translation into new surroundings would provide just the opportunity for which he was looking. We can imagine the young Henry Savile coming from the country into the great city full of hope ; a new life was about to begin

" Neither am I ignorant that I sacrifice my reputation to the persecution of implacable critics, who will find fault for custom's sake, and endeavour, by unlimited detraction, to obstruct the hopes of my parents, the end of my education, and my own endeavours."

Worst of all, he was denied the credit of the authorship of his own works, and in the case of *Sally in Our Alley* the poet tells us that :—

Because 'twas good, 'twas thought too good for mine.

From the preface to the 1729 edition of the *Poems on Several Occasions* it is plain that this was not the only work which suffered such a fate.

" Some of these offsprings of my brain," the author writes, " wandering forlorn and anonymously, were either adapted by, or assigned to, other fathers, and some good-natur'd people (I thank 'em for it), imagined 'em, homely as they are, too good to be mine." There is a broad hint at the same state of affairs in *The Poet's Resentment*, where the Muse advises him to quit writing, for :—

Determin'd to condemn thy every deed,
Thy foes have vow'd, and thou shalt not succeed ;
....

Dost thou write ill, then all against thee join ;
Dost thou write well, they swear 'tis none of thine.

Carey affected to scorn such jealousy, but his carelessness rings hollow, and is obviously forced.

His troubles, however, did not finish here for, as was the case with most successful writers of that age, he suffered extensively from surreptitious publication of his works. Piracy had existed for many years, but by the eighteenth century it had assumed vast proportions. The pirate printers were well organized, having their spies in almost every printing office in the kingdom. Richardson, who had himself suffered

18

at their hands, declared in 1753 that his friend Faulkner, of Dublin, had told him that he " had heard an Irish bookseller boast some years ago that he could procure from any printing office in London, sheets of any book printing in it, while it was going on, or before publication."[1] That piracy was profitable, the career of the notorious Curll is enough to testify, and for years a large body of unscrupulous printers had been growing fat on the stolen copies of wretched authors, who, in the absence of any adequate system of copyright, found themselves helpless against their oppressors.

In 1735 Carey complained that :—

> Pyrate Printers rob me of my gain,
> And reap the labour'd harvest of my brain.

The trouble had begun, apparently, almost simultaneously with his first appearance in print. By 1735 it had assumed tremendous proportions, how tremendous is made clear by his prefaces to *The Honest Yorkshireman*, a play written in 1735, and *The Musical Century* (1737). Inveighing against piracy in the former, he writes :—

" I have suffered very largely in this particular, nor do I live a week but I see myself injured of what would support me many months in affluence."

The Musical Century makes still more plain the lengths to which this daring robbery had been carried.

" It is almost incredible," says the poet, " how much I have suffered by having my works pirated, my loss on that account amounting to little less than three hundred pounds per annum."

All through the latter end of his life, beneath all his jollity and good humour, can be discerned an inner tragedy—the slow creeping on of poverty, and

---

[1] See *The Case of Samuel Richardson of London, Printer* (1753).

at the very time when the whole town was echoing his songs, when night after night the theatres were clattering with applause of his plays, he and his family, in their dingy house in Clerkenwell, were sinking deeper and deeper into penury. On the morning of October 4, 1743, he laid violent hands upon himself at his house in Dorrington Street, Coldbath Fields, and ended his life by hanging. In the public press it was merely stated that " he got out of bed from his wife in good health, and was soon after found dead," but the rumour of suicide is confirmed by the record of his death in the register of St. James Church, Clerkenwell, where he was buried the next day. The entry is a curious one, and reads as follows :—

> Oct. 5. Henry Carey, 56, Hanged himself.
> Charles Carey,[1] inf., Dorrington Street.

Only one interpretation appears possible ; the unfortunate man first took the life of his child, and then hanged himself. Carey left a widow and four small children " entirely destitute of any provision," for whose benefit a performance was given at Covent Garden Theatre some days later, when the famous Kitty Clive, who, as Miss Raftor, had frequently played in benefit performances for the husband, now came to the assistance of his destitute family. So passed one who, unfortunate as had been his lot, had devoted his life and genius to the amusement of his fellows, and in return had received only jealousy and ill use.

Carey started writing poetry at a very early age. His first collection was published in 1713 under the title :—

Poems/on Several/Occasions./By/Henry Carey./Inops, Potentem dum vult Imitari, Perit./London./Printed and Sold by J. Kent at

---

[1] His youngest child, Charles Colborne Carey. He was born on May 23, 1743.

the/Black Swan in St. Paul's Churchyard; /A. Boulter at the Buck, and/J. Brown at the Black Swan without/Temple Bar; and by most Booksellers. 1713./*Price* 1s./.

At this time the author could not have been more than twenty-six years of age, so that the contents of this volume are, as he describes them in the preface, " the offsprings of my youthful fancy." The success with which the book met is not apparent, but it must have proved fairly popular, for a second and augmented edition was published in 1720, while a third appeared in 1729. In 1737 the author selected some hundred of the best of his poems, set them to music, and published them as *The Musical Century*. A second edition appeared in 1740, and a third in 1743. This, briefly, is the record of Carey's poetic activity. The true bulk of his work must have been considerable, for in the preface to the 1729 edition of the poems he asserts that he had " irrecoverably lost more than double the bulk of this volume in lending my original manuscripts," and that which is still extant is no small quantity. According to Mrs. Pilkington, too, he wrote much unrecognized hack work in the capacity of " poetical stock-jobber " to Worsdale,[1] though one is naturally chary, very chary, of placing too much credence in the word of a diarist never renowned for veracity, especially as her design is to paint Worsdale in colours as black as possible.

In reading the poetry of Carey two points should be borne in mind. In the first place it is important to remember that Carey did not regard poetry as a vocation, but merely as a diversion. In the preface to the 1729 edition of the *Poems on Several Occasions*, he writes : " Poetry being my amusement, not my profession, the following pieces appear in a much worse light than otherwise they would were I less

---

[1] *The Memoirs of Mrs. Laetitia Pilkington, written by Herself*, edited by Iris Barry (1928), p. 143.

taken up with business." Secondly it is essential to bear in mind that Carey was primarily a musician and that a large proportion of the verses contained in this volume were composed to be set to music, and have often, therefore, a certain wistful, lyrical simplicity about them.

For the average reader of poetry Carey will ever remain the author of *Sally in Our Alley*, and with this piece we may open our survey of the field of his poetic endeavour. Palgrave pays it a well merited tribute by assigning it a place in the forefront of English literature on account of its " grace, tenderness, simplicity and humour," as well as for " the completeness and the unity of the picture presented." This naïve little ballad purports to be a transcript of an incident from real life, and in this respect alone it is interesting, for it assumes at once a human appeal such as is so often lacking in the average eighteenth century verse. But more than this, it is the life of the lowest classes which is here depicted, a subject quite unusual for a love lyric in the age of reason, when poetry treated mainly of the upper strata of society, or if at all it did deign to descend lower, dealt only with the same conventional characters translated into artificial pastoral surroundings, and masquerading, under the names of Strephon and Chloe, as shepherds and shepherdesses. Carey gives us something entirely different. The lover is just a simple 'prentice lad, whose master, in the true fashion of the time, used to " bang him most severely " for idling away the moments in gazing after his sweetheart. He indulged in all the boyish tricks which have ever characterized the lives of the working class, and whenever he found an opportunity, stole out of church to seek his lover, gloating over the thought that he had left his master in the lurch. The girl is equally plebeian. Her father hawks cabbage nets of his own making through the streets, while her mother sells laces " to such as please to buy 'em." Sally, too, evidently had a good appetite and a strong constitution, and like all young people was fond of plenty to eat and drink. In short, we recognize in her the typical working maid of all climes and all ages.

It can well be imagined that this idyll of simple life did arouse the derision of many of its author's friends, for to the polite world, which was mightily concerned about the dignity of the subject, and insisted that all its heroes and heroines should be of the " porcelain-clay " type, two young people such as these would appear coarse and uncouth figures for a love poem. But Carey took a broader view, and his muse, less narrow and circumscribed than those of his contemporaries, found true poetic beauty and inspiration where they would have scorned to look for them. In spite of the ridicule which was showered upon this little attempt, it nevertheless found its way into the polite world, and even the most ardent of classicists were bound to admit that it had much merit in it.

Addison's praise of Carey's work is very significant, for by reputation Addison was the most Augustan of all the Augustans, and stood for all that Carey had thrown aside. Yet though he delighted to imagine himself so strict a classicist, in one respect he was departing from the precepts of that school of literature. He had manifested a genuine interest in the popular ballad, a poetic *genre* then almost wholly neglected, and in several papers of *The Spectator* he had pressed the claims of the ballads of *Chevy Chase*, and *The Babes in the Wood*. The latter he commended on the grounds that it was " a plain, simple copy of nature," though on the other hand the verse and diction he characterized as possessing " a despicable simplicity," while the phrasing and expression were

" abject " and " poor." We can now see why " the divine Addison " vouchsafed to bestow so much praise on Carey's verses. The piece was a ballad, a poem modelled upon that popular type for the revival of which he was himself striving. It had much in common with *Chevy Chase*, while like *The Babes in the Wood*, it was " a plain, simple copy of Nature."

This unpretentious little ballad outburst of Carey's will for ever hold an honoured place in English literature. Already it has graced innumerable collections of English verse, and so long as the English language is spoken or English poetry is read will these stanzas continue to be appreciated. *Sally in Our Alley*, however, is not its author's sole contribution to ballad literature. Though generally it has remained quite unnoticed, and even by Professor Beers, a very thorough and able chronicler of the origins of romanticism, has only been accorded a passing word, Carey's name is by no means insignificant in the history of the ballad revival which characterized the early and mid-parts of the eighteenth century. *The Parish Clerk's Address*, a set of verses on the accession to the throne of George II, is written in the ballad metre, while *The Ballad of King John's Son and the Cynder Wench*, which appeared in the 1713 edition of the poems, was intended to be sung to the tune of *Chevy Chase*. At this early date, then, when his literary career was only just beginning, Carey had attested an appreciation of these old ballads, and was himself attempting to imitate them.

He was essaying in more than one direction to break away from the prevalent poetic fashions and conventions. In the year 1713 the heroic couplet was still the favourite literary form, and much of Carey's poetry is thus written in that metre, but in a number of his pieces there are to be found traces of experiments in new measures. Often he casts aside the fashionable medium and writes in a strain much more lyrical, varying the metre, the length of the line, and the *enjambement.* The following poem of two short stanzas may be taken as a typical example.

A Heart that's bleeding
With deep despair,
Is ne'er succeeding
Amongst the fair.

They hate imploring,
And courtship fly;
Each swain adoring
Is sure to die.

Rarely is anything quite like this to be found in the poetry of the Augustan age. The thought, it is true, is a fairly commonplace one in contemporary verse, but here it is not the thought but the form into which it is cast that is of importance. The chief merit lies in its straightforward simplicity and its freedom from affectation. After reading the lines of Pope and his school, with their somewhat monotonous regularity of rhythm, these stanzas come as a refreshing breath. They certainly are not characterized by very profound thinking or moralizing, but little of Carey's poetry is didactic. Pre-eminently lyrical in tone, it possesses a charm of melody quite exceptional for Augustan times ; the beauty is in the extreme felicity of expression, and the smooth simplicity of metre. Carey, remarks Hawkins, was the first to co-ordinate the two sister arts of music and poetry, and extravagant as such a statement may appear, there is no doubt that the essentially musical turn of his mind had a decided influence in attracting him away from the stereotyped couplet measure to a freer form of expression, where skilful metrical jugglery could conjure up effects incapable of being produced by the more rigid forms of verse. An excellent illustration of this is to be found in the two *Mad Songs*, where, by means of a subtle variation of metre, the author contrives to produce an atmosphere suggestive of madness and mental derangement. The rapid transition from the short to the long line, and the variation of the slow with the rapid metre, give a very strange turn to the poem. In the second of the two the lover expresses thus his sentiments upon the cruelty of his mistress :

> But I have found a way
> That shall her scorn repay.
> I'll leave this false, imaginary light,
> And seek the dismal shades of night.
> With goblins and fairies
> I'll dance the canaries,
> And demons all round in a ring ;
> With witches I'll fly
> Beneath the cold sky,
> And with the screech owl will I sing.
> My love, alas, is dead and gone,
> Is dead and gone to me,
> And now my senses they are flown,
> I have my liberty.

This type of verse is plainly the descendant of the chamber cantatas of the Italians, the object of which was, as Altisidora expresses it in D'Urfey's *Don Quixote*, to ring the changes on a number of metres, thus producing the effect of " a whimsical variety, as if I were possessed of several degrees of passion."

Lovers of Blake will doubtless regard it as sacrilege to place these verses beside Blake's *Mad Songs*, yet, though there is nothing to warrant the assumption that Blake knew Carey's poems, there is a remarkable similarity between the works and the methods of the two writers. Both have employed metrical variation to achieve their effects, both have produced a weird and supernatural atmosphere, and both have succeeded

26

in giving sympathetic expression to a mind deranged. It is perhaps noteworthy that the first of Carey's *Mad Songs* found its way into Percy's *Reliques*.

The love poetry of Carey is like the average contemporary poetry of that type, quite shallow and superficial, containing no true passion. An age which held

> Love is a medley of endearments, jars,
> Suspicions, quarrels, reconcilements, wars,
> Then peace again,

that was hardly an age to produce good amatory verses, for so cynical a view of the relations of the sexes was far from conducive to either a sympathetic or a delicate handling of the theme. The vast bulk of neo-classical erotic poetry is trivial, empty, and meaningless. Carey's is the same. It rings hollow, and true to all Augustan standards, contains little enthusiasm. The sentiment is obviously not sincere ; the treatment is purely conventional and superficial, and beneath the surface there is to be found nothing of substance. In these verses the poet was obviously writing more out of conformity to a fashion than from the emotions and feelings of his own heart.

His infallible cure for the cares of love, as indeed for all cares, is wine, and many a time does he drown his grief in " the flowing bowl."

> And now Lucinda I despise ;
> Wine, glorious wine alone I prize ;
> Wine that can all our griefs remove,
> And cure the raging pain of love.

So he concludes *The Cure of Love*. This is the entire moral of the poem *The Marriage of Bacchus*, which, ostensibly a story from Ovid, is actually a homily on the soothing power of wine. Ariadne, deserted by

27

her lover, determines to forget him, and apostrophizing his fast fading memory, exclaims :—

> Farewell, false Theseus, Bacchus now shall prove
> The only object of my constant love.

If, however, Carey treats of love but lightly, he is capable of true emotion on occasions. Eighteenth century writers showed a somewhat stoic acceptance of death. They were attracted by the outward pomp and pageantry always associated with it, but, repelled by its ugliness; they shrank from facing the thing itself. Hence in the contemporary epitaphs and elegiac poems we can detect a certain chill, classic restraint, which speaks of a tearless grief, to us to-day quite unaffecting. The eighteenth century must have had a peculiar sense of pathos. Boswell avows that Beattie's *Hermit* brought tears to the eyes of the stoical Dr. Johnson, and an age which could weep copiously over *Clarissa* was capable, in all probability, of appreciating poems which now seem rather flat and uninspired. Of the few really exquisite poems of grief produced during this age the two short elegies of Carey on the death of his child Rachel are by far the best. These beautiful little lyrics have no small merit as literary compositions. There is no doubt as to their sincerity of emotion. The poems are fraught with genuine feeling, but the author cannot quite break through the bonds of formality. The frigid lack of enthusiasm of the Augustans has checked him to some extent in the full expression of his grief, and has led him here and there into conventional turns of expression, but the pieces must nevertheless be accorded praise as poems. They rise above so many of their contemporary prototypes in that that superficiality which made use of such an occasion to produce a pretty tangle of empty sentiments is entirely absent from them. Beneath the mere words

28

there is discoverable a genuine and sincere impulse of grief.

To the expression of personal sorrow Carey brings a delicate and a skilful touch, but when he comes to depict grief in others he fails lamentably, degenerating either into mere meaningless rant and bombast, or exaggerated sentimentalism. An illustration is to be found in *The Marriage of Bacchus.* Ariadne awakens to find that Theseus has deserted her, and in grief of mind she wanders about the island of Naxos lamenting her lot.[1] But the language in which the poet describes her state cannot be termed either appropriate or affecting. It has the appearance of a burlesque rather than a faithful representation. In such situations the author's genius invariably fails him, and leads him into those bombastic utterances which he believes to signify grief, but which to the reader are the confused ravings of one demented. Yet place these pieces beside other contemporary works of a similar type, or against the agonized utterances of distressed heroes and heroines in many of the tragedies of the time, and it will be realized that Carey by no means stands alone. The inability to depict grief was an almost universal failing of the age.

In the poems on his child's death (and, indeed, in many another), it is clear that Carey is attempting to free himself from the trammels of classic formality, but he cannot quite escape. He finds that it has still some hold on him. He realizes its limitations, he aspires to higher things, yet still he feels himself unable to cast aside entirely the old strain, with its conventional epithets, its regular, rhythmical beat, and its circumscribed forms. The poem *Written in a Garden by Moonlight* promises a romantic subject, but the promise does not materialize. The moon is

---

[1] See page 52.

addressed as " Cynthia," " the beauteous rival of the darksome night," who " with transparent glories paints the sky." It shines down upon plains which are " delightful to the nymphs and to the swains." All this is strictly conventional, and could be matched in many other contemporary verses ; but a fresh touch is given when the poet goes on to describe the sporting of the lambs and the singing of the birds, who think that it is day, so brightly does the moon shine. In just such touches as these we recognize in Carey's works those new tendencies which some years later were to bear fruit in the early romantic poetry.

A favourite literary form of the early eighteenth century was the pastoral, a type of poetry which treated of rather courtly shepherds and shepherdesses, who lived in an artificially idyllic countryside, and did nothing but love, betray, and forsake each other. Ambrose Phillips (the " Namby-Pamby " of Carey's burlesque), under the influence of Spenser, had made a valiant attempt to infuse into Augustan poetry something of the sixteenth century pastoralism, but the average neo-classic pastoral was as far removed in spirit from the Elizabethan as were the pseudo-Shakespearean tragedies of Rowe from the works of the master himself. Many pastorals, mostly of the conventional kind are to be found amongst Carey's poems (*The Story of Unfortunate Phyllis* is an example), but there are just one or two which show the poet once more breaking away from his age, and introducing a note of individuality. The *Pastoral Made in the Year* 1715 is characterized by a free lyrical note, and that artificiality which mars so many others does not appear. There is also discernible in these verses the germ of that nature love which was lacking in the bulk of Augustan poetry. The tendency may be seen more highly developed in *A Rhapsody on Peace*, in which the author calls upon all created things to worship their Maker.

> Let all the various parts of Nature's voice
> In one exultant tone aloud rejoice.

This attribution of the function of worship to nature in all its forms is almost equivalent to endowing it with a soul and a divine significance, as did later poets.

The Augustan found his *milieu* in the town. His life centred around the coffee-houses, the theatre and the salon, but for all this a certain amount of plain, common-sense appreciation of the countryside was not lacking in the poetry of the time. Even the great Cowley, whom every true classicist claimed to follow, had expressed a desire for a life of rural solitude.

> My house a cottage, more
> Than palace, and should fitting be
> For all my use, no luxury.
> My garden painted o'er
> With nature's hand, not art, and pleasures yield,
> Horace might envy in his Sabine field.

Thus had he written in a set of verses *On Myself*. To the classicist, nature and the country were scarcely living realities ; he liked to turn towards them in imagination, to dwell on them in his mind, to survey them from a distance even, but probably the mental isolation and stagnation which actual contact with them would have involved would have been distasteful to him. Pope may have longed for a quiet life upon his " few paternal acres," but one cannot help feeling that his picture of the ideal existence has a strangely urban atmosphere about it, and that after all, Twickenham was more to his taste than the open, rugged countryside. Such a poem as Carey's *Mrs. Stuart's Retirement* expresses merely a vain and imaginary

31

wish. The life of the town, on the other hand, must have seemed equally attractive to the country-bred person. In *The Fine Lady's Life* Carey has once again struck a humanistic note, and in a most sympathetic manner has entered into the mind of a simple country girl, filled with ambitious dreams and aspirations. In this piece we can perhaps read some of the longings which the poet himself had felt a few years previously, when he had set out, full of hope, for the great city. Here and there, however, in spite of the more conventional touches, there flashes out a true love of the countryside. In *The Retirement* the author denounces the town, with its false and artificial life, where—

> All things borrow'd shapes and dresses wear,
> And no-one's really what he would appear,

and looks to the country as the *summum bonum*, while in *The Contented Country Farmer* he pictures his ideal life, a retired life of rural ease. This poem is perhaps the most picturesque and simple of all Carey's works. It gives us a glimpse of the poet at his happiest moments while, seated in his dreary house at Clerkenwell, he dreams of the ideal life in the country, surrounded by the fruit and flowers, and lulled by the hum of the bees.

> Near some cool stream, O let me keep
> My liberty, and feed my sheep.
> A shady walk, well lin'd with trees,
> A garden with a range of bees,
> An orchard which good apples bears,
> Where spring a long green mantel wears.

Even among the earliest romantics it would be difficult to find anything more picturesque than this stanza. The description of Spring as wearing a long green mantle is a particularly happy figure. The whole trend of the piece reminds us immediately of similar poems of Herrick. Indeed, in the poetry of Carey there is much of the Herrick strain. The earlier poet, as is well known, preached the doctrine of *Carpe diem*, and Carey's verses show the same care-free spirit. " Let us eat, drink, and be merry, for to-morrow we die," is the strain of so many of his poems.

Carey, like all the Augustans, was something of an egoist. Man is ever the centre of his poetical universe, and nature is only appreciated in so far as it contributes to human happiness or affords material comforts to mankind. The country appeals to him, not for its freedom or its natural beauty, but because it provides him with ease, luxury, and sensual pleasures.

The epicurean spirit of his verse is best seen in his many bacchanalian songs. The *Quietus*, addressed to his friend James Worsdale, and the song *Come, All ye Jolly Bacchanals* are typical examples. Wine he commends as a cure for all cares and sadness, even the malevolence of friends and rivals, and though he himself was subjected to jealousy from his fellows, he regarded it, or feigned to do so, with scorn and contempt. Thus in *Harry Carey's Reply to the Libelling Gentry*, he —

> Laughs at the malice of those who repine
> That they must swig porter, while I can drink wine.

The eighteenth century was essentially a social age, and the social spirit was reflected in the literature of the period. The poetry of Carey presents us with a series of snapshots, so to speak, of the life of the town in the lower as well as the higher strata of society. There are the court ladies and the gallants, but beside them are ranged the trading classes, the Sally Sweet-breads and the Butchers' Wives,[1] as well as the working class population, represented by Sally and her 'prentice

---

[1] Pages 125–127.

lover. In an age of Squire Westerns hunting songs would naturally abound ; thus we have such verses as *Away, Away*, or *The Morning Call to the Bride and Bridegroom*, both typical embodiments of the sporting and pleasure-loving spirit of the country gentry, whose round of life was made up of hunting during the day, and drinking at night, so that the morning after found them suffering from the effects of " the over-night cup."

Any reader of Carey's poems must be struck by the intense patriotic sentiments expressed in them. During the first few decades of the eighteenth century England was awakening to a sense of national consciousness and natural greatness. That spirit was already abroad which, some few years later, inspired a Wolfe to give his life for his country at Quebec, and a Clive to devote his energies to the establishment of English rule in the east. This spirit, symbolized in the song *God Save Great George Our King* (possibly the work of Carey himself),[1] manifested itself in literature, and gave rise to a flood of patriotic verses, many of them no more than mere " jingoism." Carey is all for England. An upholder of the constitution and the Protestant church, he despises all foreign countries. Spain and Italy especially claim his contempt. In the short poem entitled *Lysander, or The Parting*, he writes on the love and honour theme, and concludes that in times of national crisis love must give place to duty, and the lover must quit his mistress " to humble haughty Spain."[2] A similar style of poem is *The Prince of Orange's March*, in which the author attempts

---

[1] See the note to the poem on page 252.

[2] A similar sentiment is expressed in Carey's interlude *Nancy, or The Parting Lovers* (Drury Lane, 1739), in which Dreadnought, the captain of a press gang leads the youth True Blue away from his weeping sweetheart, with the words,

> Love to glory must give way ;
> Honour calls, he must obey.

to rouse his countrymen to a zealous loyalty, and to inspire a devotion to the king and royal family.

Most vehemently of all he carries his patriotic sentiments into the realms of music and the theatre. At that time the reigning passion of the town was for Italian singers and actors, who sang and spoke in an unknown tongue, and every night drew crowded houses, while English actors were quite neglected, and even despised. In *The Honest Yorkshireman*, a play written in 1735, Carey exclaims against the fabulous salaries paid to these foreigners,[1] and repeatedly in the poems he utters loud and angry protests against this invasion of the English stage. *A Satire on the Luxury and Effeminacy of the Age* is full of keen and bitter irony, but behind it all there lies a deep-grounded sentiment of pseudo-patriotism. " The Politics of Carey," says Disraeli, " were those of a poet and an Englishman." Carey was first and foremost an Englishman, and because he was an Englishman he despised all party politics. Politicians he hated, and regarded them as a selfish, designing, place-seeking company. To neither party would he own allegiance, for to him one was as bad as the other.

> I am an Englishman, and dare be free ;
> Tory and Whig are both alike to me ;
> Such shifts, such dirty work I see in either,
> I fully am determin'd to be neither.
>
> *[The True Protestant.*

His great endeavour was to infuse purity into public life, to denounce corruption, and to reconcile parties. In the poem, *Carey's Wish*, he curses corruption and bribery, and then proceeds to exhort his countrymen

---

[1] And there the English actor goes
With many a hungry belly,
While loads of gold are forc'd, God wot,
On Signor Farrinelli.

to lay aside animosities and party rivalry, and unite in an honest endeavour to make the name of England great.

> Learn, Britons, learn ye to unite ;
> Leave off the old exploded bite.
> Henceforth let Whig and Tory cease,
> And turn all party rage to peace ;
> Rouze and revive your ancient glory ;
> Unite, and drive the world before ye.

Ridicule the poet finds a weapon very useful for his purpose, and many a time does he lash " the cunning politician, whose aim is to gull the people."

Travesty, satire and burlesque occupied a conspicuous place in Augustan literature, and it was this spirit which most clearly manifested itself in Carey. In this connection two of his poems require a special note. *Namby-Pamby* is interesting if only for the fact that it added to the English language the two very expressive words which form its title. It was first published in 1725 as *Namby-Pamby, a Panegyric on the New Versification, Address'd to A—— P——, Esq.*

A—— P——, Esq., despite the attempts of an anonymous contemporary writer to prove his identity with Alexander Pope,[1] was Ambrose Phillips, now chiefly remembered for his pastorals and his quarrel with Pope. The appellation " Namby-Pamby," it is needless to explain, is a childish diminutive of that poet's name. Phillips had acquired a habit of writing poems in a simple style, and in short lines, to the children of the nobility, with the object, it was then rumoured, of ingratiating himself with the flattered

---

[1] See the Second Edition (1727) of *Pudding and Dumpling Burnt to Pot*. This small pamphlet claimed to be a key to an anonymous treatise published in the previous year and entitled *A Learned Dissertation on Dumpling*. It seems probable that both the original *Dissertation* and the key were written by Carey himself. The question is treated at length in the present writer's article *An Eighteenth Century Original for Lamb ?* printed in *The Review of English Studies* for October, 1929.

parents, and so obtaining a lucrative post. For our present purpose one in particular, addressed to the infant daughter of Lord Cartaret, is important. A few lines from the opening of the poem will serve to illustrate the style.

> Pow'r o'er every pow'r supreme,
> Thou the poet's hallow'd theme,
> From thy mercy seat on High,
> Hear my numbers, hear me cry.
> Breather of all vital breath,
> Arbiter of life and death,
> Oh, preserve this innocence,
> Yet unconscious of offence,
> Yet in life and virtue growing,
> Yet no debt to nature owing.

A cursory reading of these lines will immediately convince one that Dr. Johnson was by no means overstating the truth when he remarked that they " are not loaded with much thought." They certainly are not. Carey had always been a champion of simplicity in poetry, but the style of lines such as these of Phillips was a degenerate form of simplicity. They were mawkish and puerile, and Carey could see their stupidity. Always a good imitator, in a moment of facetiousness he strung together a number of short, jingling lines, exactly in the manner of Phillips, which burlesqued admirably that poet's efforts, and raised a universal shower of derision against them. Into the poem he has woven all the well-known nursery rhymes and infantile tags, so that the result is a masterpiece of parody. It proved very popular, and numerous imitations appeared, while Pope, who was himself never tired of satirizing Phillips, substituted the appellation " Namby-Pamby " for the poet's real name wherever it occurred in his works.

Greatly to the author's annoyance this poem, like so many others of his works, was attributed to any pen but his own. It was Pope, apparently, who first discovered the real author and established his claim, for in the epistle *Of Stage Tyrants* Carey declares that :—

> Common fate did various authors chuse
> To *Namby-Pamby*, offspring of my muse ;
> Till Pope, who ever prov'd to truth a friend,
> With gen'rous ardour did my cause defend ;
> Trac'd me obscure, and in detraction's spite,
> Display'd me in a more conspicuous light."

Incidentally it would be interesting to know more of Pope's relations with Carey and his chivalrous behaviour upon this occasion, for his name is not usually associated with actions of so disinterested a character.

Carey's other important satirical work is the epistle *Of Stage Tyrants*, valuable not only as a satire, but also for the light that it throws upon the relations of the author with the theatre and the world of letters. In 1735 he wrote his ballad farce, *The Honest York-shireman*. It appears that originally he offered the piece to Drury Lane Theatre, but the management, after keeping the copy for many months, refused to act it, and returned it to the author at a time when it was almost too late for him to place it with any other company. Finally, however, it found a refuge at Goodman's Fields, where it enjoyed a run of several weeks. But Carey's troubles did not end here, for, proving so successful, the play was immediately pirated and published as *A Wonder : An Honest Yorkshireman*. In the preface to the authentic edition which appeared some few weeks later, the author complains bitterly of his treatment at the hands of theatre managers and publishers. After inveighing against " the bad taste and the monstrous partiality of the Great Mogul of the Hundreds of Drury," he continues :—

" Time was when masters of playhouses dreaded

the displeasure of the town ; now they put the publick to defiance, use authors and actors just as they please ; silence, discourage, suppress at pleasure, copying Sadler's Wells instead of Greece and Rome, so that we must have double prices and puppet shows whether we will or no."

On the subject of piracy he has much to say :—

" Of all pyracies that of this farce was the most flagrant and impudent, for, impatient to stay till I had publish'd my own copy, they villainously and surreptuously anticipated me, thereby robbing me of a considerable sum, and imposing on the publick not only a false and spurious edition, but at double the cost I ever intended."

So incensed was Carey at his treatment by the Drury Lane management that in a fit of anger he penned the epistle to Lord Chesterfield, *Of Stage Tyrants*, a vigorous attack on Fleetwood, the manager of the theatre. It appeared in folio in November, 1735. Fleetwood seems to have had the unfortunate habit of offending everyone with whom he came into contact. Amongst his victims was Mrs. Charlotte Charke, the actress daughter of Colley Cibber. Mrs. Charke's play, *The Art of Management*, is a satire hardly less severe than Carey's epistle. In it the proprietor of Drury Lane is represented as the theatre manager, Brainless, who creates such a fiasco that ultimately he is forced to resign his position.[1] The attack on Fleetwood in *Of Stage Tyrants* is of a nature rather different from that of Mrs. Charke's play. Carey had a personal injury to avenge and a hurt pride to satisfy. Though the piece is ostensibly an

---

[1] Benjamin Victor gives an account of Fleetwood which is anything but laudatory. " Duplicity," he remarks, " was the prevailing characteristic of Mr. Fleetwood " (*History of the Theatres of London and Dublin*, 1761, Vol. I, p. 63). A lengthy account of the quarrel with Mrs. Charke, slightly embroidered by the author, no doubt, is given in *The Narrative of the Life of Mrs. Charlotte Charke, Written by Herself* (1750).

attack on stage tyrants, the satire is not confined to Fleetwood alone. For years now Carey had been smarting under the ungenerous behaviour of his rivals and the literary world in general. For a long while he had succeeded in hiding his annoyance, but once roused to anger, he was unable to restrain himself. All his old quarrels rankled afresh in his mind, and he lashed right and left unsparingly. Not only are persons ridiculed, but whole classes of drama are satirized. Pantomime was a type which was fast usurping the place of the regular play, and though it was popular with the town, and brought in large profits to managers, it was manifestly unpopular with writers, who found their own efforts rejected in favour of this innovation.[1] Pantomime is scathingly condemned by Carey, and is stigmatized as :—

But a pompous puppet show at best.

This epistle reveals a new aspect of Carey's character which, in many ways, we would wish to overlook, for here he is no longer " the facetious Harry Carey." Instead he shows up as petulant, conceited, and jealous. In this work there appears a tinge of petty spite, and personal, malicious rancour. His more fortunate fellow writers he brands as " handy hirelings," and accuses them of plagiarism, in that they :—

Steal a new ballad-farce from some old play.

The charge is true enough. Many of the popular Ballad Operas were merely old farces furbished up, and brought into line with the prevailing taste ; or

---

[1] Pantomine, an English development from the *commedia dell'arte*, is to be connected with the eighteenth century Italian cult, and in his condemnation of it Carey seems to have recognized this connection. It gained a footing on the English stage in the last few years of the Restoration period, when Italian Opera was also first introduced, but the person chiefly instrumental in its popularization was John Rich, or Lun, as he called himself, who made a reputation in the part of Harlequin.

often they were re-workings of a hackneyed plot with stock characters ; but the fact is quite irrelevant to Fleetwood's tyranny. Carey has here deliberately digressed from the main drift of his satire to censure his contemporaries in a manner which savours of petulance in the extreme. He himself was, after all, by no means free from the faults which he condemns in others, for many of his dramatic works are merely copies of the scores of similar productions which were daily appearing on the boards of the London theatres.

He contrasts the present condition of Drury Lane Theatre with that during the period when it was under the management of Wilks, Booth and Cibber, and again his wounded pride prompts him to give vent to an outburst of petty spite. In a somewhat peevish tone he contemplates quitting dramatic composition, since the " trifling farces " of " upstart witlings " are preferred to his own plays. He is, of course, unable to conclude the poem without his usual complaint against piracy, and soundly does he trounce the " pyrate printers," who

> . . . rob me of my gain,
> And reap the labour'd harvest of my brain.

" As a poet," declares one critic, " Carey was the last of that race of which D'Urfey was the first." This does him less than bare justice, for the two men cannot stand even in the same category with each other. In the collection, *Pills to Purge Melancholy*, hardly a single verse can be called decent ; D'Urfey, a true son of the Restoration, delighted in the obscene and the prurient. But against Carey this charge can never be levelled. With all his joviality he never transgresses the bounds of modesty nor violates decency. In fact he actually condemns some of the more common pleasures of the time as vicious. In spite of the tone of his many Bacchanalian songs, excessive drinking

41

can never be charged against him, for we have it on the authority of his friends that though " the facetious Harry Carey " was always a pleasant companion, he was but moderate in indulgence in his pleasures. In the age of Anne and the first two Georges excessive gambling was the favourite pastime amongst all classes. The king and the court set the fashion, and the rest of the country followed the royal lead. The fever assumed tremendous proportions, ranging from speculation in South Sea Stock and the wholesale political bribery of Walpole to the ventures of the quadrille table, and many a family as old as that of Castlewood found itself ruined by gaming. The vice was even given national sanction by a state lottery! Such a vogue, however, did not go quite unchallenged. Churchmen attacked it, of course, but literature also took up the cudgels on behalf of morality. Mrs. Centlivre raised her voice against it in her comedy *The Gamester* (1705), while two years later Colley Cibber wrote in the same strain in *The Lady's Last Stake*, and with these Carey joined forces, producing such a piece as *The Effects of Gaming*, in which he curses cards and dice as disseminators of vice, discord, and domestic misery. In such a poem we see Carey the moralist, tinged with that spirit of sentimentalism which was fast making itself felt in English literature.

In his attitude towards the female sex, too, he stands in contrast with the average writer of the time. While the majority of contemporary poets and dramatists regarded women as faithless, fickle creatures, full of every imaginable vice, and wicked and adulterous by nature, he stoutly champions them, and never refers to them but with marked deference, and in terms of great respect. In the ballad of *Sally in Our Alley* he had depicted a " chaste and disinterested passion " in a young 'prentice and his lover. At one time a rumour was circulated that the heroine of the poem was a certain Sally Salisbury, a woman of very doubtful reputation who led a debauched life amongst the gallants of the town, but upon this statement coming to Carey's notice he indignantly refuted what many another writer would have regarded as of little consequence, and hastened to assure his readers that " innocence and virtue were ever the boundaries of his muse." Innocence and virtue he certainly always maintained in his attitude towards women. In the two short poems, *The Happy Marriage* and *The True Woman's Man*, he pictures the ideal wife,

> A constant lover and a faithful friend.

Even in his own time it was recognized in some quarters, not without commendation, that to him woman was a much more sacred and much purer being than to the majority of writers. In an epilogue spoken by Mrs. Cantrell to his play, *The Honest Yorkshireman*, the actress makes an appeal to the ladies present to show their approval, and to applaud the play as the author has always been their champion and stood up for their rights :—

> Ladies, I now must plead the poet's cause ;
> He's your old champion ;—shall he have applause ?
> If value for our sex can recommend,
> He's known by all to be a woman's friend."

This insistence upon the rights of women and the sanctity of the marriage state connects him with the movement for sentimentalism which, inaugurated at the end of the previous century by Colley Cibber, and fostered by Steele, was rapidly becoming noticeable in the drama, though it was by no means without its influence on other branches of literature also. Sentimentalism, which was born of the same parent as the nature philosophy of Jean-Jacques Rousseau, and paved the way to the romanticism of the later years of

43

the century, is at bottom, according to Professor Bernbaum, "a confidence in the goodness of average human nature." Its aim was a moral one, to show virtue triumphant over vice, and to extol the virtuous life. Now the poetry of Carey is marked by all these characteristics. The goodness of average human nature is his constant theme. His object, too, is avowedly a moral one. In *Of Stage Tyrants* he declares that :—

> To please and yet instruct is all my aim,

and then proceeds to condemn those poets and dramatists

> Whose only view is to corrupt the taste,
> To soothe the vicious, and to shock the chaste.

The condemnation of gaming and its attendant vices is in the same moral tone, and points in a similar direction. Sentimentalism meant ultimately the destruction of all social barriers, and already in the literature of the early eighteenth century a tendency in that direction is visible. In his comedy, *The King and the Miller of Mansfield*, Dodsley preached the revolutionary doctrine of "A man's a man for a' that," a doctrine voiced also by Carey in *The Surly Peasant*, where he exclaims :—

> A Fig for your Sir or your Madam ;
> Our origin all is from Adam ;
> Then why should I buckle,
> Palaver, or truckle
> To any pragmatical chuckle ?

Carey, it has been remarked, is now one of the forgotten worthies of literature. For many years his name, overshadowed as it has been by those of his greater and better known contemporaries, has remained in obscurity, yet in his own day he was one of the most successful and best known of writers, and his works enjoyed a popularity of which many a less fortunate rival was profoundly envious. In 1735 he himself declared that :—

> My little ballads still on ev'ry tongue
> Are in politest conversation sung,

and, judging from contemporary records, he was by no means overstating the case. Isaac Disraeli, writing some hundred years later, when the poet's great grandson, Edmund Kean, was drawing crowded houses by his acting of Shakespeare, pays a warm tribute to Carey. Says Disraeli, " He could neither walk the streets, nor be seated at the convivial board, without listening to his own songs and his own music,—for in truth, the whole nation was echoing his verse, and crowded theatres were applauding his wit and humour."[1]

There is much that is interesting in the works of Carey, which, in spite of their faults (and they are numerous), have in them many qualities of permanent value. They are notable first and foremost for the spirit of democracy and broad humanitarianism by which they are characterized, a spirit which cannot fail to appeal to any lover of poetry. If, as Professor Oliver Elton alleges, " he had a truly Thackerayan gift for little rhymes,"[2] in his attitude towards the common people he is Dickensian. Carey was a human figure in an essentially artificial age. Possessed of the keen and penetrating insight of the satirist, he saw how hopelessly divorced from life and reality was much of the literature of the time, and it was his aim to bring the two into closer contact. Tradition has it that on

---

[1] Isaac Disraeli : *Calamities of Authors,* (1881), page 101.

[2] Oliver Elton : *A Survey of English Literature,* 1730–1780, (1928), Vol. I, page 282.

the very eve of his death, when he was beset on all sides with poverty and distress, he launched a fund for the support of decayed musicians. That was characteristic of the man. He was keenly interested in humanity, and it was that interest which gave so felicitous a touch to many of his verses. Scarcely anything else of the time is to be found to equal, for its human appeal, his ballad of *Sally in Our Alley*. From its first appearance to the present day, for a period of two hundred years, this little poem of the love of a 'prentice lad has endeared itself to the hearts of Englishmen from the highest to the lowest.

Together with this humanitarian spirit, and closely allied to it, goes a certain sincerity and simplicity. More than once did Carey attack the artificiality of his age, and plead for a wider outlook. He saw that the only hope of literature's becoming once more invigorated was for it to lay aside its conventions and limitations, and to orientate itself in the direction of a more simple mode of expression. He was never afraid to treat of the life and ways of the common people, for many a time did he go to " low life " for his subject, and in so doing he gave expression and impulse to a new, growing spirit in the realm of literature, a spirit of broad sympathies and democratic feeling, which was eventually to give rise to the poetry of Burns and Wordsworth.

POEMS OF HENRY CAREY

THE MARRIAGE OF BACCHUS

Being part of the Story of Theseus and Ariadne
Imitated from Ovid

THE ARGUMENT

Theseus, sentenc'd to be devour'd by the Minataure,
is preserv'd by Ariadne, daughter of Minos, King of
Crete, who for love of Theseus, and fear of her father's
fury, flies by night with Theseus to Naxos, where he
treacherously leaves her, and retires with her sister
Phaedra to his father's court at Athens.

The following poem leaves part of the story to be
understood, and begins at daybreak, after the flight
from Crete, and the first sight of Naxos.

At length the joyous morning's welcome light
Began to shoot through that propitious night,
Which veil'd the heav'ns, and screen'd their con-
  scious flight,
When bright Aurora issu'd from the east,
In all her gaudy robes of daylight drest,
And, in an instant, open'd to their view
The finest landscape nature ever drew.
'Twas plenteous Naxos, the belov'd abode
Of wine's most potent, most luxuriant god ;
Which, scarce beheld, but leaping from the main,
As it were glad to rest itself again,
The ship cut swiftly through the yielding sand,
And lodg'd its burden on the wish'd-for land.

Then safety smil'd in ev'ry gladsome face ;
They blest themselves, and hail'd the happy place.
For why ? . . .

The dire revenge of Minos most severe
Had fill'd their guilty souls with so much fear,
They had despair'd to wish, much more to meet
With so secure, and such a sweet retreat.
Amid the gloomy horrors of the deep,
What soul, tho' most fatigu'd, could think of sleep?
There was no rest; but Naxos can supply
Those blessings which the boist'rous seas deny.
The swelling vines here blow themselves in haste,
And grapes in purple clusters court the taste:
Promiscuously around, of ev'ry kind,
A wild desert of rip'ning fruits they find:
They're nature's guests, nor can they wish for more,
When she so freely lavishes her store.
Through plenteous wilds of gay confusion led,
With easy steps they gain a fountain's head,
Whose streams of liquid crystals swiftly roll
Around the margin of the verdant bowl,
While on each side the spreading beeches seem
To kiss the clouds, and shade the glitt'ring stream.

Thus ev'n beyond their expectations blest,
'Tis here they gladly lay 'em down to rest
On flow'ry pillows, and on verdant beds,
While quiv'ring branches rustle o'er their heads;
And close beneath the gentle murm'ring streams
Charm them to softest slumbers, sweetest dreams.

But, ah! while beauteous Ariadne sleeps,
Thoughtless of ill, the faithless Theseus keeps
A treach'rous watch, and real slumber feigns,
Tho' waking falsehood in his bosom reigns;
For soon as he perceives her killing eyes
Securely veil'd, he gently does arise,
And with the slowest motion lightly moves,
To find the maid whom he unjustly loves.

This done, with hasty joy the guilty pair
Fly to the ship, and with officious care
All hands do for their instant flight prepare.
Propitious winds soon fill their swelling sails,
The sable streamers sport with friendly gales,
The well stirr'd rudder ploughs the wat'ry plain,
Swifter than thought they fly along the main,
And soon the distant shore of Athens gain.

While Ariadne, lull'd to peaceful dreams,
Like some bright angel in a slumber seems ;
Upon a pillow which the earth had made
Of rising turf, her head was gently laid ;
The blushing roses stoop'd on either side,
And strove to kiss her cheeks with eager pride.
But, ah ! they droop'd, and pale with envy grew,
To see in them a more vermilion hue.
The lilies, that on either side did grow,
And in their whiteness rivall'd whitest snow,
Clos'd their fair heads, within their folds retir'd,
And, vanquish'd by her whiter skin, expir'd.

Meantime great Bacchus, with his jovial train,
In savage triumph came along the plain ;
A spotted panther, drunk with lees of wine,
Reeling and foaming drew the car divine ;
A crowd of Bacchae ran on either side,
Their bloated cheeks with juice of elders dy'd,
As many laughing satyrs, row by row,
With wanton motion skipping to and fro ;
While old Silenus, jogging in the rear,
Did slowly creeping on an ass appear.

It chanc'd at last that Bacchus bent his way
Unto the place where Ariadne lay,
But Heav'ns ! with how much wonder did he gaze !

His train stood still, and all were in amaze
To see that unfrequented, lonely place
Blest with so sweet a form, and so divine a face.

The god was fixt, as rooted to the ground ;
No motion in his greedy eyes was found :
He gaz'd as though he would exhaust his sight,
And seem'd all fill'd with rapture and delight.
The wanton satyrs peep'd, and smil'd, and skipt,
Around the fair a thousand times they tripp'd ;
Yet, cautious lest they should the nymph affright,
They talk'd in whispers, and their steps were light.

At last the god drew nigh, and gently laid
His sacred body near the sleeping maid ;
While she in dreams, not knowing he was there,
Embrac'd him, call'd him Theseus, and her dear ;
She press'd his hand, and to augment his bliss,
She, slumb'ring, met his face, and stole a kiss.
Great Bacchus, ravish'd with the balmy taste,
With too, too eager joy the nymph embrac'd,
Who, starting from his arms, began to wake,
And, gazing, found too late the sad mistake.
She shriek'd, and leaping from the grassy bed,
She tore the golden tresses from her head ;
Aloud she call'd for Theseus, but alas !
He, like a faithless wretch, had fled the place ;
She beat her breasts and wept, but all in vain ;
Theseus was gone, ne'er to return again.

Now here, now there she flies in wild despair,
Her locks dishevell'd streaming in the air ;
She seeks the shore, and finds the vessel gone,
And then, O Heav'ns ! with what excessive moan
She fill'd the place. Within the briny sea
She would have plung'd, but Ah ! that might not be ;
She was prevented by the god of wine,

Who, full of pity, us'd his pow'r divine
To calm her stormy soul, to ease her pain,
And place her reason on its throne again.
But deaf to all the pleading pow'r could say,
She stopt her ears, and would have forc'd away.
'Tis thou, said she, with fury in her eyes,
Hast made my dear lov'd lord a sacrifice !
Can'st thou not kill me too, that I may go
And seek him in the peaceful shades below ?

The god with patience heard the frantic fair,
With pity saw her anguish and despair ;
He told her Theseus' falsehood, and the maid
Who had her lover from her arms betray'd.
Scarce had she heard, when Lo ! her spirits fail,
Convulsive throws her tortur'd soul assail ;
Bacchus, in pity, takes her to his arms,
And by his pow'r recall'd her pristine charms.

He told her of his passion and his truth,
His pow'r divine, his never dying youth ;
He let her know the falsehood of mankind,
And of the pleasures she wou'd daily find
Within his arms. He told her she wou'd reign
O'er him, his island, and o'er all his train.
He knelt, he begg'd, he wou'd not be deny'd,
She blush'd and smil'd, and with a sigh reply'd,
Farewell, false Theseus, Bacchus now shall prove
The only object of my constant love.

The god stood ravish'd at her matchless charms ;
He clasp'd the yielding fair one in his arms ;
The leaping satyrs did with joy rebound,
The Bacchae lightly touch'd the trembling ground ;
Loud *Ios* fill'd the place, and ev'ry voice
Was heard in gladsome transports to rejoice ;
E'en nature's self look'd more sublimely gay
To solemnize great Bacchus' nuptial day.

THE FIRST DISTICH OF CATO PARAPHRAS'D

Si Deus est animus nobis ut carmina dicunt,
His tibi praecipue sit pura mente colendus.

    If that almighty, infinitely good
And glorious power, who, when all things stood
On nothing, and were nothing, gave command
So efficacious, that no helping hand
Assisted, to compose the spacious world,
But ev'ry atom in its place was hurl'd ;
At whose despotick word . . . .
Night from its gloomy prison issu'd forth,
The teeming womb of chaos brought forth earth,
And gave the sun, the day, and ev'ry being birth

    If this so good, so great, so glorious pow'r
Who was before all things at this hour,
Whom we call God, be, as we have been told
By the inspired, learned men of old,
A form of purest and divinest air,
Beyond conception, and without compare,
Stupendously glorious, in whom all
Those heavenly graces mortles virtues call
Shine so conspicuous that their dazzling rays
Dim my aspiring soul, and bid my lays
Forbear with bold attempt to sing his praise,

    Then let each human soul with awful fear,
With holy love and contrite heart appear
Before yon Heav'n, his blest abode, and pray
Late in the night, and early in the day
To him, the only object of our vows,
Who all our secret thoughts and wishes knows.

Nor let the powers of sloth and pride
Permit his sacred image e'er to slide
From our serenest thoughts, but let us keep
It fix'd awake, and dream of it in sleep :
Thus may we keep our God within our soul,
And all immoral thoughts and deeds controul.

THE SECOND DISTICH OF CATO
PARAPHRAS'D

Plus vigilia semper, nec somno deditus esto ;
Nam diuturna quies vitiis alimenta ministrat.

Since thou, O happy man, alone art blest
With heavenly knowledge, since thy glowing breast
With such celestial raptures is inspir'd,
And all thy godlike faculties are fir'd
With the reflection of the heaven-born mind,
Whose boundless scope no eye but God's can find ;
Thy mind the express image of thy God,
Which can in highest Heav'n take its abode,
Tho' this vile earth contain the viler clod.

Permit not, then, the baleful type of death
Insensibly to steal your sense and breath ;
Nor let the drowsy pow'r presume to keep
Thy soul a captive in injurious sleep
One moment past the time that nature grants
T'afford the rest thy wearied body wants.
As many hours you from sleep refrain,
So many hours of new life you gain ;
Therefore from all immod'rate rest abstain.

Nor suffer an inglorious ease to waste
That precious time which passeth too, too fast
To be recover'd. Can you dare to throw
Away a gift God only can bestow,
On needless trifles ? Shall thy godlike soul
Which can ascend from glitt'ring roof and roll
In wanton ecstasies from pole to pole,
Be spent and wasted in a thoughtless ease,
And ne'er employ'd but menially to please
Some wanton thought ? Nor yet invok'd to sing
A theme beyond a mistress . . .
When it should always praise the heav'nly King.

Then fly with greatest fear from luxury,
From sleep, from sloth, those keys to misery ;
Those hot-beds in which vices grow so fast,
And which destroy mankind with so much haste
That, when he would repent, the time is past

A PASTORAL ECLOGUE ON THE DIVINE POWER OF GOD

Spoken by two Young Ladies in the Habits of Sherperdesses, at an Entertainment Perform'd at Mrs. Carey's School by Several of her Scholars

SERAPHINA

Now say, my dear, if Seraphina's glade
Is not for pleasure and retirement made ?

DODONA

I willingly confess it, and rejoice
In Seraphina's company and choice.

SERAPHINA

What, then, forbids that we should jointly raise
Our blooming fancies, and employ our lays
To sing and celebrate our Maker's praise ?

DODONA

What can forbid when inclinations move,
When we are prompted by seraphick love ?
When in a glade so pleasant, so retir'd,
That I believe myself to be inspir'd.

SERAPHINA

'Tis then your right, Dodona, to begin,
For surely one inspir'd can better sing
Than such a thoughtless, simple maid as I ;

DODONA

Leave, Seraphina, leave your raillery.
Tho' of yourself you humbly may conceive,
I know too well to say I but believe
You have a soul short only of divine,
In which such wond'rous excellencies shine,
They far exceed each nymph's, much more
Inferior mine. . . .

SERAPHINA

Is this the language of a country maid!
'Tis fitter for a court than for a glade:
Forbear, my dear Dodona, since you know
My thoughts are humble, and my station low,
Then should not my discourse and life be so?
We came not here to praise ourselves, but Him
Whose wond'rous goodness is a boundless theme.

DODONA

Forgive me, Seraphina, and begin;
You challeng'd first, and you the first should sing

SERAPHINA

Tell, nymph, by whom this most delightful shade,
These lovely greens, these fragrant flow'rs were
made;
By whom we live and move, say, nymph, who gives
A source to all our thoughts, and nurture to our
lives?

DODONA

That sacred pow'r whose boundless essence rolls
Far, far above the skies, as far beyond the poles,
He gives a verdant tincture to the fields,
And all these various dyes which nature yields:

He fills the bank with violets, and bestows
A fragrant odour to the blushing rose :
By Him our tender lambs are taught to bleat ;
He gives the motion to their nimble feet.
In short, birds, beasts, and ev'rything that moves.
Thro' realms aerial, or terrestial groves ;
Fishes and monsters, whatsoe'er they be
That sport in crystal streams, or salter sea ;
Being unknown, unseen, each thing and all
We may the most minute existence call,
Whether in Heav'n or air, or sea, or land,
Were fram'd by God's omnipotent command,
Who still upholds the same ; for still they bear
The mark of their Creator's pow'r and care.

SERAPHINA

That bounteous God, Dodona, is the theme
On which my tongue, like fruitful Nilus stream,
Could now, and ever, flow with grateful praise
To Him of whom the very thoughts can raise
My rural muse much more sublimely high
Than any heathen bard can dare to fly.

DODONA

But O, my Seraphina, is not He
A subject too sublime for you and me ?

SERAPHINA

How dare you doubt the goodness of the Lord ?
He is not yet too great to be ador'd :
For O, He shows in the most lively sense
His mercy, equally His omnipotence ;
Else had mankind been punish'd for their sin,
Else had this world a second chaos been ;

But He, supremely good, supremely wise,
Sits high enthron'd, and with indulgent eyes
Beholds his creatures bow, and hears them breathe
Their grateful thanks, and songs of praise beneath.
When Phoebus at the morning's dawn displays
O'er all the earth his bright, his genial rays,
All creatures rouse to bless the infant sun,
And nature puts her gayest habits on.

A golden lustre crowns the mountain's heads,
And gives a splendour to the painted meads ;
A brilliant warm profusely fills the fields,
And silver streams a dazzling brightness yield ;
A splendid tincture gilds the laden trees,
And shines triumphant in the glitt'ring seas.

Thus ev'ry morn, with charms entirely new,
Nature prepares for the Almighty's view ;
Who, full of mercy and of pleasure sees
The stately lion bend his kingly knees,
And bow with humble zeal his awful head ;
While subject brutes, by his example led,
Declare with eyes elate, and bended knee,
They feel within themselves the God they see.

This done, the whole creation does prepare,
With grateful sounds to charm its Maker's ear :
And now all beings vigorously join
To make the entertainment more divine.

Now chirping birds, whose tender pinions bear
The flutt'ring songsters thro' the yielding air,
In loudest, sweetest strains, essay to sing
Eternal anthems to their heavenly King.
Then ev'ry species takes its proper part ;

But Oh, the utmost pitch of human art
Or pow'rful rhetorick can ne'er express
That killing harmony, that soft excess,
That soul of musick, nature's charming voice,
Which makes both God and man and all rejoice

If, then, to please their God all beings join,
Why should distinguish'd we alone decline,
Tell me, O, tell me, dear Dodona, why
Should we alone despise celestial majesty ?

DODONA

Forbid it, Heav'n ! and Thou, eternal God,
Who dwell'st in yon empereal abode,
Forbid that anything proceed from me
Offensive to Thy sacred majesty.
Come, Seraphina, join with me in pray'r,
Our joint petitions God will surely hear ;
His sacred pardon freely he'll dispense,
Since ignorance occasion'd my offence.

SERAPHINA

But see, the day begins to disappear,
And darkness with her gloomy train draws near ;
Night now ascending in a sable shade
Begins to veil the heav'ns ; and dark the glade ;
Then come, my dear Dodona, haste away,
We safer now may in our cottage pray.

DODONA

Bless me ! how we've beguil'd the hours away !
Here's not the smallest glimpse of cheerful day ;
That sun which lately smil'd on ev'ry field,
Is now in Thetis' watery lap conceal'd ;

The sable vestment of thick darkness shrouds
The azure beauties of the lofty clouds ;
The lambkins to their cotes affrighted run,
The meads in which they sported now they shun ;
The warbling songsters of the feather'd choir
To their warm nests securely now retire.
The gloomy shades that fill this hateful place
Make all things here to wear another face ;
Then home let's fly on swiftest wings of fear,
For nought but horror smiles on all things here.

AN EPILOGUE TO THE SAME
ENTERTAINMENT

Spoken by a Little Boy

Ladies, . . .

The happy time of peace draws near,
Europe no more the yoke of war shall wear ;
Great Anna will a lasting peace obtain,
To crown the wonders of her glorious reign.[1]

Then, O ye pensive fair, lament no more,
Your lovers soon will gain the British shore ;
They'll leave the fields of war for peaceful plains,
Proud to be call'd your ever constant swains ;
To you they will resign their glitt'ring arms,
As the just trappings of your conquering charms,
But, . . . as you tender my advice . . . be kind,
And let your heroes no resistance find,
Lest they, enrag'd to see you cruel prove,
Should wage a war instead of making love.

Ev'n I myself will arm in such a cause,
And make you yield to Cupid's pow'rful laws ;
I'll head the men of courage, wit, and parts,
And then, disdainful nymphs, have at your hearts.

But if you'll strictly follow my advice,
You all shall have good husbands in a trice.

Let virtue be your guide in all your ways,
'Tis virtue gains alone esteem and praise ;
Vice may awhile ensnare a worthless heart,
But virtue gains without the help of art ;
And she whom virtue's sacred laws inspire
Shall still enjoy whate'er she can desire.

PROLOGUE TO *THE RIVAL QUEENS,*

OR

THE DEATH OF ALEXANDER THE GREAT[1]

Acted at a boarding school by young ladies

How mad are we in so refin'd an age
To ape the tragic muse, and tread the stage !
But all that for this folly can be said
Is that we act for pleasure, not for bread.
We, for the while, disclaim our teacher's rule,
And to a theatre transform our school.
Our forms and benches rang'd commodiously
Serve us for pit and box and gallery ;
Tap'stry supplies the place of painted scenes,
While we, imaginary kings and queens,
Strut in heroics,[2] dizzen'd in attire
Compos'd of feathers, spangles, lace, and wire ;
So, if we chance to fail, some recreation
You'll surely find in such a transformation.
But since we've none but friends assembl'd here,
Why should we tremble ; what have we to fear ?
If in our childish pastimes we should miss,
You have more manners, surely, than to hiss :
For what can you expect from such as we
But virgin blushes and simplicity ?
Consider, we have none our cause to aid ;
Our very Alexander is a maid.
Then on our youth some tender pity take,
And spare the action for the actors' sake.

PROLOGUE ADDRESS'D TO THE LADIES

*Intended to be Spoken by little Miss Robinson at her
Benefit*

To whom can innocence for succour sue,
Or hope protection, ladies, but from you?
From you whose breasts with gen'rous pity glow,
Whose eyes for others' sorrows kindly flow.
What, not a hiss?   (*Looking about
                No woman hater here?*
We'll have no plaister'd pates tonight, I fear;
No Petits Maîtres, who themselves admire,
And rob the ladies ev'n of their attire.
Oh, that I could but have my will, I'd teach 'em
To make such splutter about Polly Peachum!
Well, let 'em take their Polly and their fancy,
So I, dear ladies, could but be your Nancy,
And this your Polly.   (*Introducing her sister*
                Cheer the infant pair,
And bless us with your smiles, ye British fair.
Sister, with serious air and shape most taper,
                   (*Mocks her sister*
Shall tread sublimely, while I attempt a caper.
        (*Cuts a caper and shews Harlequin tricks*
Thus diff'rent ways we'll strive to give delight,
Inspir'd by the appearance of the night.
Our only study now shall be to please,
By you upheld, still bright'ning by degrees,
While such a circle of the brave and fair
Adorn our house, and take us to their care.

EPILOGUE

Spoken by Mr. Cibber, Junior, 1729[1]

If language could our grateful thoughts express,
Those thoughts should want not for poetic dress ;
But words, Alas ! are far too poor to show
The thanks we to your kind indulgence owe,
Who've merit made of our desire to please,
Wink'd at our faults, and rais'd us by degrees ;
Encouragement, the very life of art,
Stirs up the active mind, and fires the heart,
From small beginnings makes th'industrious mend,
And struggle, till perfection crowns the end.
Accept our humble thanks for favours past,
And give us hopes to think 'em not the last :
In pity pardon what has been amiss,
Another year may mend the faults of this ;
And if hereafter we deserve applause,
Be yours the praise, whose goodness was the cause.

SUNG BY MRS. CLIVE

In " Columbine Courtezan "[1]

Crowds of coxcombs thus deluding,
Cringing, chatt'ring, oggling, flatt'ring
By coquetting and by pruding,
All are victims to my art.
While at will the fools I'm leading,
They for favours interceding,
With vain hopes their fancies feeding,
Still untouch'd I keep my heart.

Each imagines he shall gain me,
Thinks I prize him, who despise him ;
All their wiles shall ne'er obtain me,
Born to baffle all mankind.
Like the winds and waves still changing,
Never constant, ever ranging,
Cupid from my heart estranging,
That's as cold as he is blind.

THE FINE LADY'S LIFE,

OR

THE THOUGHTS OF AN AMBITIOUS COUNTRY GIRL ON THE PLEASURES OF THE TOWN

Sung by Mrs. Cibber in " The Provok'd Husband "[1]

What tho' they call me country lass,
I read it plainly in my glass,
That for a duchess I might pass,
Oh, could I see the day !
Would fortune but attend my call,
At park, at play, at ring, at ball,
I'd brave the proudest of 'em all,
With a stand by, . . . clear the way !

Surrounded by a crowd of beaux,
With smart toupets and powder'd cloathes,
At rivals I'll turn up my nose,
Oh, could I see the day !
I'll dart such glances from these eyes,
Shall make some nobleman my prize,
And then, . . . Oh, how I'll tyrannize !
With a stand by, . . . clear the way !

Oh, then for grandeur and delight,
For equipage, for diamonds bright,
And flambeaux that outshine the light,
Oh, could I see the day !
Thus ever easy, ever gay,
Quadrille shall wear the night away,
And pleasures crown the growing day,
With a stand by, . . . clear the way !

THE ROMP'S SONG

Sung by Mrs. Cibber in " The Provok'd Husband "

Oh, I'll have a husband, ay marry,
For why should I longer tarry
Than other brisk girls have done ?
For if I stay
Till I grow grey,
They'll call me old maid,
And fusty old jade ;
So I'll no longer tarry,
But I'll have a husband, ay marry,
If money can buy me one.

My mother she says I'm too coming,
And still in my ears she is drumming
That I am too young to wed.
My sisters they cry
Oh fie, and Oh fie !
But yet I can see
They're as coming as me ;
So let 'em have husbands in plenty ;
I'd rather have twenty times twenty
Than die a despis'd old maid.

THE INTRIGUE

A Dialogue

To be sung in " The Country Wake"[1] *by Mr. Ray and Miss Raftor, in the characters of Friendly and Flora*

Make haste and away, my only dear,
Make haste and away, away !
For all at the gate your true love does wait,
And I prithee make no delay.

Oh, how shall I steal away, my love,
Oh, how shall I steal away ?
My daddy is near, and I dare not for fear ;
Pray come, then, another day.

Oh, this is the only day, my life,
Oh, this is the only day ;
I'll draw him aside, while you throw the gates wide,
And then you may steal away.

Then prithee make no delay, dear boy,
Then prithee make no delay ;
Let's serve him a trick, for I'll slip, in the nick,
And to my true love away.

Chorus

O Cupid, befriend a loving pair,
O Cupid, befriend us, we pray.
May our stratagem take, for thine own sweet sake,
And Amen let all true lovers say.

EPILOGUE INTENDED FOR MR. CIBBER'S NEW PASTORAL CALL'D *LOVE IN A RIDDLE*[1]

To the Tune of "Sally in Our Alley"

Since singing's grown so much in vogue
    With this harmonious nation,
'Tis fit we suit our epilogue
    Unto your darling passion.
Then from the courtier to the cit,
    As France has done before us,
Let box, let gallery and pit
    All bear a bob in chorus.

We want, Alas, the voice and gift
    Of charming Senesini ;
Permit us, then, to make a shift
    With Signor Cibberini.
What tho' his lays he cannot raise
    To soft Cuzzoni's[2] treble,
Like Chaucer's clerk our tuneful spark
    Can squeak a sweet quinible.

To please the town a thousand shapes
    Like Proteus he does borrow ;
A fop or clown today he apes,
    A cardinal tomorrow.
Thus human nature he does trace
    Thro' all its various fashions,
And suits his actions, voice, and face
    To diff'rent parts and passions.

As is the darling looking-glass,
    Of fops the sole direction,
So of the gentleman or ass
    A player's the reflection.

71

For as his character he suits,
    In diff'rent lights he shows you
The mighty odds 'twixt men and brutes,
    T'instruct, and not expose you.

Thus in this retrospect of life
    You see mankind in little ;
'Twixt worth and scorn the constant strife,
    And worldly joys how brittle ;
How hateful vice is, spite of bags,
    Of grandeur and oppression,
While truth and virtue, tho' in rags,
    Are lovely past expression.

As goes a bear unto the stake
    An actor treads the stage-a ;
His spirit sinks, his heart does ache
    For fear of critics' rage-a ;
For they are such mischievous elves,
    And so delight in riot,
They neither will be pleased themselves,
    Or let mankind be quiet.

Oh, yield not up poor Colley's play
    To party rage and spite-a,
Since he endeavours ev'ry way
    To give the town delight-a ;
You sav'd his last from envy's blast,
    Spare then in pity this-o,
But one poor night, in mere despite
    Of those who come to hiss-o.

EPILOGUE TO *THE PURITAN,*
OR
THE WIDOW OF WATLING STREET[1]
Spoken by Miss Young, who played the part of Molly

Unable in that hateful state to tarry,
I thought 'twas best to chuse a fool, and marry.
The pure ones will, I know, with outstretch'd voice,
Arraigne my judgement, and condemn my choice :
But what could I ?   I strove with might and main
To keep the temper from me, but in vain ;
The spirit weaken'd, and the flesh grew stronger,
So, to be short, I could hold out no longer.

Accordingly I took my goodly spouse
To be a movable about the house ;
To pay my debts, to father what I bear,
And let him say against it if he dare.
O ladies, ladies, marry while you may ;
Consider you grow older ev'ry day.
A husband is a necessary evil,
But chalk and coal and oatmeal are the devil.

Let no-one here admire that one so young
Should to such ripen'd subjects turn her tongue ;
In ages past, indeed, 'twould wonder raise,
But these, you know, are most experienc'd days.
Now little miss in hanging sleeves knows more
Than formerly her grandame at three score ;
And master, who was lately whipt at school,
At bare fifteen sets up for rake and fool,
Runs the whole race of vice with full career,
Is green, and ripe, and rotten in a year.
And should seven ages more, by swift degrees,
Render our youth sevenfold more ripe than these,
In marriage bands we must our infants swaddle ;
They'll woo and wed before they leave the cradle

THE HAPPY NUPTIALS[1]

DAPHNIS : GERON

GER : How comes it, Daphnis, that our nymphs and
swains
With more than usual joy and gladsome strains
Thus wildly wanton frolick in excess,
Unknowing how their transports to express ?

DAPH : Can any Briton ask ? . . . But thou art old,
And to life's gaieties entirely cold,
Or thou had'st known that from the Belgic
shore
A royal stranger late is wafted o'er ;
Never was Albion with a nobler grac'd,
In whom the gods have ev'ry virtue plac'd.

GER : You speak his praises like the voice of fame ;
But has this miracle of men no name ?

DAPH : Of ancestors heroic, race divine,
Illustrious branch of the Nassovian line ;
William his name, from mighty William
sprung,
Of whose immortal deeds great Prior sung.

GER : No wonder, then, that universal bliss
Succeeds th'arrival of a prince like this ;
Nassau, the very name does joy inspire,
And renovates my soul with youthful fire :
What instinct from the kindred god above
Induc'd his blest arrival ? . . .

DAPH :   Powerful loe ;
Fir'd with the fame of royal Anna's charms,
What could withhold her from his longing
arms ?

Seasons and seas in vain his way oppose,
For such a bride who would not life expose ?
In whom all virtues, all perfections join,
A form angelic, and a soul divine,
To grace whose nuptials nature's self looks
   gay,
And night illumin'd brightens into day.
E'en winter now becomes another spring,
In honour to the daughter of our king.
Quite lost in joy behold the gladsome throng ;
All haste to hail them in a rural song ;
See in what pompous pleasures they advance,
And to Sicilian measures nimbly dance ;
Young Lycidas, the chorist, tunes his lays
In joyful epithalmick to their praise ;
The chorus aids him with exulting voice,
While Heav'n applauds our transports and
   their choice.

Air I. Lycidas

Thrice welcome royal stranger,
To greet thee see all nature smile,
Whom Neptune, free from danger,
Has wafted to our isle.
            (Chorus : *Thrice welcome*, etc.

Air II

By Anna's charms invited,
Nassau defies the sea ;
In Anna's charms delighted,
What god so bless'd as he !
            (Chorus : *Thrice welcome*, etc.

Air III

May ev'ry joy attend 'em
No end their sweet endearments know,
And bounteous Heav'n befriend 'em
With all it can bestow.
            (Chorus : *May ev'ry joy*, etc.

THE PRINCE OF ORANGE'S MARCH

Sung by Mr. Hulett in " Britannia "[1]

Brave grenadiers, rejoice
With gladsome heart and voice ;
For fair Britannia's choice
Your martial sports prepare.
Let silver trumpets sound,
Let brazen drums rebound,
While shouts of joy fly round
To hail the happy pair.

Forgot are war's alarms
Within the fair one's arms,
For Venus' powerful charms
Can mighty Mars subdue.
May all the gods above
Reward their constant love,
And may they ever prove
Still happy as they're true.

THE NUPTIAL DAY

Illustrious pair, by Heav'n design'd,
The pride and pleasure of mankind,
Nature your virtues does approve,
And bids the lifeless statues move.
See, they seem to breathe and live,
And to your love their plaudits give,

Come, tune your pipes, ye jovial swains,
And fill the air with cheerful strains.
Trip, trip, ye nymphs, the circle round,
And light as zephyrs touch the ground.
Sing, sing and dance, rejoice and play,
'Tis fair Britannia's nuptial day.

THE WEDDING DAY

Sung by Master Osborne[1] in " The Happy Nuptials "[2]

Cupid, god of gay desires,
Hymen with thy sacred fires,
Smiling zephyrs haste away,
Grace this happy nuptial day.

Loves and graces all attend,
Pow'rs propitious all befriend,
Make them your peculiar care ;
Bless this happy, happy pair.

SONG IN *BRITANNIA*

He comes, he comes, the hero comes,
Sound your trumpets, beat your drums ;
From port to port let cannons roar
His welcome to the British shore.

Prepare, prepare, your songs prepare ;
Loudly rend the echoing air ;
From pole to pole your joys resound,
For virtue is with glory crown'd.

AN ODE PRESENTED TO HER MAJESTY
ON HER BIRTHDAY

Darling of Heav'n, and glory of the earth,
Illustrious Anna, whose auspicious birth
To Britain's welfare gave a happy date,
And bless'd us with a goddess to our queen,
For surely such are you, in whom is seen
All that is good, and ev'rything that's great.

Best of your sex, and best of monarchs too,
What praises to your name are due !
What songs to Anna shall we sing ?
What pyramids erect, what off'rings bring ?
Shall we in soft, harmonious lays
Attempt to celebrate your praise ?
Or shall the muse and voice unite their charms,
To sing the glories of your reign, the conquests of
    your arms ?

Ah ! No, in vain, Alas ! we strive to find
So bright a genius, so elate a mind,
Whose daring muse on steady wings may glide
Thro' realms celestial with triumphant pride,
And, with stupendous fury, boldly wrest
The teeming raptures from an angel's breast.

No wonder, then, if such a muse as mine
Should cease to aim at subjects so divine ;
For Ah ! her tender pinions ne'er can fly
Thro' realms so insuperably high.

Since, then, the languid muse her aid denies,
My supplicating soul shall scale the skies,
And for your welfare earnestly implore
The sacred three in one whom we adore ;
While all your subjects in my prayers shall join,
That God would make you happy, as you are divine.

A LILLIPUTIAN ODE ON THEIR MAJESTIES'
ACCESSION

Smile, smile,
Blest isle !
Grief past,
At last,
Halcyon
Comes on.

New King,
Bells ring ;
New Queen,
Blest scene !
Britain
Again
Revives
And thrives ;
Fear flies,
Stocks rise ;
Wealth flows,
Art grows.
Strange pack
Sent back ;
Own folks
Crack jokes.
Those out
May pout ;
Those in
Will grin.

Great, small,
Pleas'd all.
God send
No end
To line
Divine
Of George and Caroline.

THE PARISH CLERK'S ADDRESS ON THE SAME SUBJECT

In the Style of Hopkins and Sternhold

The parish clerks of fair London,
  Whose hall in Wood Street stands,
Leige subjects all, and ev'ry one,
  Crave leave to kiss your hands.

When that your father he was dead
  We did lament full sore ;
But since that you are in his stead
  Right glad we are therefore.

God bless your noble majesty,
  Your queen and children all ;
And send that no adversity
  On you or yours befall.

May you of church and realm take cure,
  Of clergy eek and lay ;
And may your reign and fame endure
  For ever and for aye.

VERSES FOR THE USE OF THE BELLMAN OF FULHAM

Written after his own Style,
Being a Prayer for the King and Royal Family

O God, preserve his sacred majesty,
And also bless the royal family ;
As for his enemies, O Lord, down pull 'em,
But bless my masters all that live at Fulham.
Let ev'ry sick man there become a well man,
And send them store of crop to tip the bellman.

LYSANDER, or THE PARTING

RECIT.

Lysander brave and young,
Withheld by her whom more than life he priz'd,
And who for him all other youths despis'd,
E'er to the wars he did repair,
Thus address'd the weeping fair
With broken sighs and falt'ring tongue.

AIR

Who can to war's alarms
Fly from those folded arms ?
Yet that must I.

O Cupid, god of love,
Would'st thou propitious prove,
Here let me die.

RECIT.

While thus entranc'd he stood,
The silver trumpet from afar
Chides his delay, and calls to war :
New vigour fires his blood,
His soul is all alarm'd, he starts, he flies,
And to the trumpet's call he thus replies :

AIR

Sound, sound to arms, away, away,
Bellona calls, I must obey.
Yet 'tis hard fate to leave thee so,
But honour calls, and I must go.

A LOYAL SONG

Sung at the Theatres[1]

God save great George our King,
Long live our noble King ;
  God save the King.
Send him victorious,
Happy and glorious,
Long to reign over us ;
  God save the King.

O Lord our God arise,
Scatter his enemies,
  And make them fall.
Confound their politicks,
Frustrate their knavish tricks ;
On him our hopes we fix ;
  O, save us all.

Thy choicest gifts in store
On George be pleased to pour ;
  Long may he reign.
May he defend our laws,
And ever give us cause
To say with heart and voice,
  God save the King.

CAREY'S WISH

Curst be the wretch that's bought and sold,
And barters liberty for gold,
For when election is not free
In vain we boast of liberty.
And he who sells his single right
Would sell his country if he might.

When liberty is put to sale
For wine, for money, or for ale,
The sellers must be abject slaves,
The buyers vile, designing knaves ;
It has a proverb been of old,
The devil's bought but to be sold.

This maxim in the statesmen's school
Is always taught, *Divide and Rule.*
All parties are to him a joke ;
While zealots foam he fits the yoke.
When men their reasons once resume,
'Tis then the statesman's turn to fume.

Learn, Britons, learn ye to unite.
Leave off the old exploded bite ;
Henceforth let Whig and Tory cease,
And turn all party rage to peace.
Rouse, and revive your ancient glory ;
Unite, and drive the world before ye !

THE SATYRIST

Sure none but an ass
To humour a lass
Would ever be kept in subjection ;
For if she's unkind,
Her scorn never mind,
But leave her, and wean your affection.

Some women, 'tis said,
Like Hebrew are read ;
Each look should be took quite contrary ;
For subject to change,
And fond of what's strange,
Like the wind and the sea they will vary.

All, all is disguise,
Their hearts and their eyes ;
They'll flatter you while they deceive you ;
But let them secure
You once in their lure,
Ten thousand to one but they leave you.

A BALLAD ON THE TIMES

A Merry land ! By this light
We laugh at our own undoing,
And labour with all our might
For slavery and ruin.
New factions we daily raise,
New maxims we're ever instilling,
And him that today we praise
Tomorrow's a rogue and a villain.

The cunning politician,
Whose aim is to gull the people,
Begins his cant of sedition
With *Folks, have a care of the steeple !* [1]
The populace this alarms,
They bluster, they bounce, and they vapour ;
The nation's up in arms,
And the devil begins to caper.

The statesmen they rail at each other,
And tickle the mob with their story ;
They make a most horrible pother
Of national interest and glory.
Their hearts are as bitter as gall,
Tho' their tongues they are sweeter than honey ;
They don't care a fig for us all,
But only to finger our money.

If my friend be an honest lad
I never ask his religion ;
Distinctions make us all mad,
And ought to be had in derision ;

They christen us Tories and Whigs,
When the best of 'em both is an evil ;
But we'll be no party prigs ;
Let such godfathers go to the devil.

Too long they have had their ends
In setting us one against t'other,
And sowing such strife among friends
That brother hated brother.
But we'll for the future be wise,
Grow sociable, honest, and hearty ;
We'll all of their arts despise,
And laugh at the name of a party.

THE METHODIST PARSON

Ye parsons of England who puzzle your pates,
Who hunt for preferment, and hope for estates,
Give over your preaching, your hopes are but small,
For the Methodist parson has out-cut you all.

What signifies learning and going to school,
When the rabble's so ready to follow a fool ?
A fool did I say ? No, his pardon I crave ;
He cannot be fool, but he may be a knave.

For all his fine whim-whams, Alas, are no more
Than what his friend Mahomet practis'd before ;
Now mark what I say, and you'll find I say true,
Tho' religion's the cry, ready money's the view.

Don't history tell how the fair maid of France
Led all that whole nation the very same dance ?
So slyly the gipsy cock'd up the affair,
The poor Dauphin himself was drawn into the snare.

You all may remember the fam'd Mother Map[1]
Who flourish'd at Epsom, and made such a rap ;
Some thought her an angel, some thought her a witch,
Till she roll'd from her chariot, and dy'd in a ditch.

In religion, as well as in physick, we find
That quacks have the art of bamboozling mankind.
The age is roll'd round o'er a new forty-one,
'Tis high time that new sectaries should be begun.

But let them alone, and they'll dwindle away,
As they rose of themselves, of themselves they'll decay ;
At first they astonish, at last they're a joke,
For they burst forth in flames, and they vanish in
    smoke.

THE UNION OF PARTIES

A Churchman and Dissenter
Had once an odd adventure,
And grew exceeding hot.
They made a mighty pother,
And railed at one another
About they knew not what.

But when they came to cooling,
And leave off party fooling,
They found they'd been to blame
Like Christian and like brother
They look'd at one another,
For each man meant the same.

That names of Whig and Tory
Were all an idle story,
A stateman's artful snare ;
Invented to divide us
But with a view to ride us,
And then the cash to share.

That trade and navigation,
Those bulwarks of the nation,
We should with life defend ;
And not with tame subjection
Be subject to inspection,
Or to proud Spaniards bend.

So reconciliation
Succeeded disputation,
Both being in one mind.

To make their hearts the lighter
They made their cheeks the brighter,
And in this health they join'd.

A Protestant Succession,
Without the least oppression
In Church or yet in State.
O may our faith's defender
Increase the nation's splendour,
And make us truly great.

THE RAT TRAP,

OR

THE WAY TO CATCH A POLITICIAN

AN EPIGRAM

Qui Capit, Ille Facit

With hand on double heart and uplift eyes,
The sly, designing politician cries,
" For my dear country's sake I toil all day,
And wear in tedious thought the night away."
Now, if aright this man I understand,
'Tis for his own dear country house and land.

THE PLAGUE OF DEPENDENCE

Courtiers' words let no man mind,
They vary like their fashions ;
They bamboozle all mankind
To please their darling passions.
Would you be wise
And endeavour to rise,
You must nothing consult but their pleasure ;
That's a sure and only way
All your labour to repay,
With a snack of the publick treasure.

Let the tradesman tend his shop,
And not turn politician ;
Let the farmer mind his crop,
Content with his condition.
As for a place,
'Tis a palpable case,
You may dance out your shoes in attendance ;
There are candidates enow,
So you'd better go to plough,
Than to wait for a court dependence.

A HUE AND CRY AFTER M . . . K,

LATE MASTER TO A CORPORATION IN THE CITY OF DUBLIN

By the Author of " Namby-Pamby "[1]

A master of late,
Ah! hear the sad fate
Which many men say will attend him.
They say his condition
Wants no mortal physician,
So the devil I've pitch'd on to mend him.

This master did strive,
For no man alive
Was equally fir'd with ambition.
Not Croesus himself,
Nor six times his pelf
Should coax me into his condition.

An old founder'd mare,
Once as fleet as a hare,
His name is, they say, Corporation,
He gain'd to bestride her,
But how he did ride her,
Read that in his own reputation.

No honest man, sure,
Would ever endure
Such damnable heaps of conviction.
Though he would persuade
Ev'ry man of his trade
What all can allege is a fiction.

91

This mare, till he rid her,
Ne'er leaned on her wither,
But soberly trotted and gallop'd.
But he only maul'd her,
Poor creature, and haul'd her,
To make his own kettle to wallop.

But to cover the cheat
He threw out a bait,
A new fangl'd law he invented,
Which he thought the poor mare,
Us'd to moderate fare,
Would have easily have been contented.

But the honest men all,
Who paid for her stall
In which this mare should be attended,
Soon found out the cheat,
And closely debate
That her stall and her tackle be mended.

This her master, 'tis true,
Was able to do,
If honesty had been within him.
But t'have told him of this,
'Tis 'gainst thunder to piss,
For only the devil can win him.

His head is still running
On tricking and cunning,
But he mayn't escape, let me tell you ;
For the fox has been caught,
And pay'd dear at last,
For the geese he has put in his belly.

The fox might escape
For this monstrous rape,
Were the geese given into his charge ;
And might fairly have nick'd 'em
And cunningly trick'd 'em,
But here is manslaughter at large.

If the cries of the poor
Every day at his door
Can't soften his noddle, nor melt him,
May the blackguard of town
Gain some little renown,
And with pellets of perjury pelt him.

THE GRUMBLETONIANS,

OR

THE DOGS WITHOUT DOORS

A FABLE

A wealthy farmer in the west,
With life's enjoyments amply blest,
A man esteem'd both far and near,
Who in his house kept . . . special beer !
Twelve children eek around his table,
All lusty, lively, brisk and able.

He carried wond'rous well his age,
His wife was housewifely and sage ;
They throve, and pick'd up wealth apace,
And none of them at church took place.

Two mastiff dogs he kept to guard
His house, his poultry, and his yard,
Whose hungry paunches well he fill'd,
With offal from the meat he kill'd.
All sleek they were, and in good case,
Which shew'd the plenty of the place.

But in the house they durst not enter,
My dame her crock'ry would not venture,
For she had tea-table and china,
And held her head as high as any ;
Her house was kept too nice and neat
For dogs to traipse with dirty feet.

For many years these currs were quiet,
Nor grumbled at their bounds or diet ;

Would bark at beggar or at stranger,
And make much noise at little danger ;
But to the comers to and fro
No marks of surliness they'd shew.

A hound the farmer had beside ;
A hound, his heart's delight and pride.
Peerless he was of all his kind,
So fleet, he would outstrip the wind ;
The best that ever follow'd game ;
Frolick he was, and Fly his name.

Caress'd and lov'd by ev'ry soul,
He rang'd the house without controul.
This made the angry mastiffs jealous,
Fly should be rais'd above his fellows,
Keep his nose warm, and lick the plates,
While they stood shiv'ring at the gates.

They grudge each, but that goes beside 'em,
And vow revenge, whate'er betide 'em ;
At last so wond'rous curst they grew,
At friend and foe alike they flew.

These ugly currs kept such a rout,
No mortal durst stir in or out ;
To quell their rage their master try'd,
But they his threats and him defy'd ;
Nor would their fury be abated ;
They bark'd the more the more he rated,
And made such a confounded din,
For quiet sake he let 'em in :
For why, the noise disturb'd the head
Of my good dame, now sick in bed.

No sooner was the wicket ope
But both into the kitchen crope,
Wagging their tails, all tame and mild
As harmless lamb, or sucking child.

These currs, who were so fierce before,
Now crouch and wriggle on the floor,
Fawn at the very servants' feet,
And tremble lest they should be beat.

They next traverse the kitchen round,
To see what prog is to be found ;
Where, having fed to heart's desire,
They stretch themselves before the fire ;
Content and snug they lay till broad daylight ;
The house was still, my dame slept well that night.

MORAL

Thus fares it with the discontented race,
Who envy others when in pow'r and place ;
They rail, they write, they plot, but all the rout
Is not for who is in, but who is out ;
Let 'em but have a finger in the pye,
They change their tone, and give themselves the lye.

A SATIRE ON THE LUXURY AND
EFFEMINACY OF THE AGE

Capillum frangere, et ad muliebres vocem extenuare,
mollitie corporis certare cum fœminis, et immundissimis
se excolere munditiis ; nostrorum adolescentium specimen
est. (Sen. Rhet. Controv. I.)

Britons ! for shame, give all this folly o'er,
Your ancient nobleness restore :
Learn to be manly, learn to be sincere,
And let the world a Briton's name revere.

Let not my countrymen become the sport
And ridicule of ev'ry foreign court ;
But let them well of men and things discern,
Their virtues follow, not their vices learn.

Where is the noble race of British youth
Whose ornaments were wisdom, learning, truth ?
Who, e'er they travell'd, laid a good foundation
Of lib'ral arts, of manly education ;
Nor went, as some go now, a scandle to their nation,
Who travel only to corrupt the mind,
Import the bad, and leave the good behind.

To learning and to manly arts estrang'd,
As if with women sexes they'd exchang'd,
They look like females dress'd in boy's attire,
Or Salmon's waxwork babies, propp'd with wire ;[1]
And if a brace of powder'd coxcombs meet
They kiss and slabber in the open street.

Curse on this damn'd Italian pathic mode,
To Sodom and to Hell the ready road !
May they, when next they kiss, together grow,
And never after separation know.

Our Petits Maîtres now are so polite
They think it ungenteel to read or write.
Learning with them is a most heinous sin,
Whose only study is to dress and grin,
To visit, to drink tea, gallant a fan,
And ev'ry foolery below a man.

Powder'd and gumm'd the plaister'd fop appears,
The monkey tail hangs 'twixt the ass's ears,
Just emblem of the empty, apish prig,
Who has more grin than grace, less wit than wig.
'Stead of a sword their person to secure
They wear a bodkin rather, or a skewer,
But with a tossil of prodigious make,
To show they wear the weapon for the top-knot's sake.

Saucy and pert, abrupt, presumptive, loud,
These shadows triumph o'er the vulgar crowd ;
But let a man of sense and soul appear,
They fly before him like the tim'rous deer ;
For, be they ne'er so healthy or so young,
Their courage only lies upon their tongue.

They talk not of our army and our fleet,
But of the warble of Cuzzoni[2] sweet,
Of the delicious pipe of Senesino,[3]
And of the squalling trull of Harlequino,
Who, were she English, with united rage
Themselves would justly hiss from off the stage.

With better voice, and fifty times her skill,
Poor Robinson[4] is always treated ill :
But such is the good-nature of the town,
'Tis now the mode to cry the English down.

Nay, there are those as warmly will debate
For the academy as for the state ;
Nor care they whether credit rise or fall ;
The opera with them is all in all.
They'll talk of tickets rising to a guinea,
Of pensions, duchesses, and Bononcini ;[5]
Of a new eunuch in Bernardi's[6] place,
And of Cuzzoni's conquest or disgrace.

Not but I love enchanting music's sound
With moderation, and in reason's bound ;
But would not for her syren charms reject
All other business with supine neglect.
When leisure makes it lawful to be gay,
Then tune your instruments, then sing and play.
Musicians, I shall give what you deserve,
Yet will not let all other artists starve ;
But even deal with a more lib'ral hand
To him who sings what I can understand.

I hate this singing in an unknown tongue ;
It does our reason and our senses wrong ;
When words instruct and music cheers the mind,
Then is the art of service to mankind ;
But when a castrate wretch of monst'rous size
Squeaks out a treble, shrill as infant's cries,
I curse the unintelligible ass,
Who may, for ought I know, be singing Mass.

Or when an Englishman, a trimming rogue,
Confounds his English with a foreign brogue,
Or spoils Italian with an English tone,
(Which is of late a mighty fashion grown),
It throws me out of patience, makes me sick ;
I wish the squalling rascal at Old Nick ;
Far otherwise it is with honest Dick.[7]
Like Clytus he, with noble Grecian pride,
Throws all unmanly Persian arts aside,
Sings when he's ask'd, his singing at an end,
He's then a boon, facetious, witty friend.
How much unlike those fools who sing or play,
Yet for themselves have scarce a word to say ;
Who shall one moment with their music please,
The next with stupid conversation tease.

But above all those men are most my jest
Who, like uncleanly birds, bewray their nest.
When Englishmen implicitly despise
Their own produce, can English merit rise ?
Nipp'd in the bud, nor suffer'd once to blow,
How can it ever to perfection grow ?

Yet erst for arts and arms we've been renown'd ;
Our heroes and our bards with garlands crown'd ;
Are we at last so despicable grown
That foreigners must reign in arts alone,
And Britain boast no genius of her own ?

Can then our British syrens charm no more,
That we import these foreign minstrels o'er
At such expense from the Italian shore ?
Are all our English women ravens grown ?
And have they lost their melody of tone ?
Must music's science be alone deny'd
To us, who shine in ev'ry art beside ?

Is then our language grown a very joke,
Not fit by human creatures to be spoke ?
Are we so barbarous, so unpolite ?
We but usurp superior merit's right.
Let us to them our wealth, our dwellings yield,
To graze with savage brutes in open field ;
And when we've learn'd to squeak Italian, then,
If they so please, we may return again.

Is music, then, of such importance grown
All other knowledge must be overthrown ?
Let, then, the learned judge resign the bench
To some fine singer, some Italian wench.
Let the divine forget the labour'd text,
With tones and semi-tones to be perplex'd ;
The merchant, too, regard his trade no more,
But learn to sing at sight, and write in score ;
Let us forget our ancient, barb'rous speech,
And utter nought but what Italians teach ;
Let's send our useless dross beyond the sea,
To fetch polite Imperial and Bohea ;
Let our toupets to such a length extend
That vanquish'd France shall copy, but not mend ;
And Italy itself be forc'd to say
We fiddle and we sing as well as they.

THE POET'S RESENTMENT

Occasion'd by some Persons doubting the Author's
Capacity, and denying him the Credit of his own Works

Resign thy pipe ! Thy wonted lays forego !
The muse has now become thy greatest foe.
With taunts and jeers and most unfriendly wrongs
The flaunting rabble pay thee for thy songs.
Untuneful is our native language now,
Nor must the bays adorn a British brow.
The wanton vulgar scorn their mother tongue,
And all our home-bred bards have bootless sung.
A false politeness has possess'd the isle,
And ev'rything that's English is old style.

Ev'n heaven-born Purcell now is held in scorn ;
Purcell, who did a brighter age adorn.
That nobleness of soul, that martial fire
Which did our British Orpheus once inspire
To rouse us all to arms is all forgot ;
We aim at something . . . but we know not what.
Effeminate in dress, in manners grown,
We now despise whatever is our own.

So Rome, when famous once for arts and arms,
Betray'd by luxury's enfeebling charms,
Sunk into softness, and its empire lost ;
We may be as refin'd, but to our cost.

Then break thy reed, for ever close thy throat,
Nor dare to sing a line, nor pen a note,
Since any other man shall meet with praise
For what from thee will but derision raise.
Determin'd to condemn thy ev'ry deed
Thy foes have vow'd, and thou shalt not succeed.

Go, seek retirement, learn to be obscure ;
The wretch that's least observ'd is most secure ;
Dost thou write ill, then all against thee join ;
Dost thou write well, they swear 'tis none of thine.
Short liv'd applause is stifl'd soon as born,
While nought subsists but envy, censure, scorn.
The jest of coxcombs, ev'ry fool's disdain,
These, these are the rewards of poets' pains.
Far, far away, then, chase the harlot muse,
Nor let her thus thy noon of life abuse ;
Be busy, know no joy but sordid pelf,
And wisely care for no man but thyself ;
Mix with the common crowd, unheard, unseen,
And be thy only aim the golden mean ;
And if again thou tempt the vulgar praise,
May'st thou be crown'd with birch instead of bays.

An epistle to the Right Honourable Phillip, Earl of Chesterfield, Occasion'd by " THE HONEST YORK-SHIREMAN " being rejected at Drury Lane Playhouse and since acted at other Theatres with Universal Applause

O Chesterfield, my patron and my pride,
In whom does all that's great and good reside ;
Noble by birth, by liberal arts refin'd,
Delight of Heav'n, and darling of mankind ;
The publick patriot and the private friend,
To curb th'oppressor and th'oppress'd defend,
To hated indolence no more impute
The muse's silence, if hereafter mute ;
She quits her former toils for future ease,
And checks that genius which, perhaps, might please.

'Tis time my fruitless labours to decline,
When all men's work can climb the stage but mine ;
When, in my stead, behold a motley herd
Of upstart witlings to myself preferr'd.

Not so when Booth, Wilks, Cibber rul'd the stage,[1]
Dramatick ornaments of this our age ;
My small attempts to please were then approv'd,
And not for ev'ry trifling farce remov'd.
Booth ever shew'd me friendship and respect,
And Wilks would rather forward than reject.
Ev'n Cibber, terror of the scribbling crew,[2]
Would oft solicit me for something new.

Now younger rulers younger authors take,
Not for their merit, but for cheapness' sake ;
These handy hirelings can, in half a day,
Steal a new Ballad Farce from some old play,
To mangl'd scraps of many an ancient tune
Tagg feetless jingle, jarring and jejune ;
The jaded players with equal haste rehearse,
Till sing-song limps to horrid, hobbling verse.

Tho' blunder follows blunder, line by line,
The squire is taught to think 'tis wond'rous fine.
It suits his taste, he gives his plaudit voice,
And shows his understanding in his choice,
Framing conceptions both of men and things
Just as Sir Figg directs his leading strings.

Sir Figg, grand master of the double sneer,
Who, when he most deceives, seems most sincere ;
Dissembler born, but much improv'd by art,
A friendly aspect, an infernal heart ;
The mischievous, the busy go-between,
Easy squire Amb's-Ace, and fly Harlequin ;
Who, like two wrangling counsellers at bar,
In publick seem to contradict and jar,
But yet in private like dear friends caress,
And form designs poor players to distress.

Woe to the stage if once their schemes succeed ;
Actors will then be abject slaves indeed :
Poets had better lay their pens aside
Than tamely truckle to stage tyrants' pride.
Who, vain and partial, keep old authors down,
To force their own low trump'ry on the town.

Why to such wretches should I yield my cause,
So lately honour'd with so much applause ?
My little ballads still on ev'ry tongue
Are in politest conversation sung ;
Nor can severest censure trace one line
That tends to vice in any verse of mine.
To please and yet instruct is all my aim,
Let venal poetasters boast the same,
Whose utmost views are to corrupt the taste,
To sooth the vicious, and to shock the chaste,
And quite estrang'd from any sense of shame,
Make women speak what rakes wou'd blush to name ;
Then in excuse plead nothing else goes down—
A wretched compliment upon the town.

Wretched as false—The town's not so deprav'd,
Were authors and were actors less enslav'd ;
Could one good piece be suffer'd to appear
The town would gladly lend a candid ear ;
Prefer pure nature and the simple scene
To all the monkey tricks of Harlequin :
The Man of Taste[3] proves this assertion true ;
We want what's rational as well as new.

But this declension of the British stage
Booth, Britain's Roscius, justly did presage ;
That rules dramatick, humour, taste, and wit
Must to that monster Pantomime submit ;
Yet Pantomime, in all its grandeur drest,
Is but a pompous puppet show at best.

Then farewell stage ! Be business now my boast,
With what was irksome, once delighted most ;
Pleas'd and contented with my little store,
I scorn to prostitute my muse for more.

Alas ! what fame, what gain can I propose,
When others father fast as I compose ?
To such a pitch is pert presumption grown,
'Tis well if this poor piece be thought my own.
So, when long since, in simple sonnet lays,
I made the 'prentice sing his Sally's praise[4]
Tho' rude numbers, yet the subject mov'd ;
Immortal Addison the lay approv'd ;
Then prejudice with envy did combine ;
Because 'twas good, 'twas thought too good for mine.

So common fate did various authors chuse
To *Namby-Pamby*, offspring of my muse,
Till Pope, who ever prov'd to truth a friend,
With gen'rous ardour did my cause defend ;
Trac'd me obscure, and in detraction's spite,
Display'd me in a more conspicuous light.

To mention more wou'd prove a needless task.
Why should they not be mine ? that's all I ask.
Beacause I'm chearful, unreserv'd, and free,
Can nothing good or new proceed from me ?
What have I done injurious to mankind,
My works must be to other men assign'd ?

Well, let 'em go, I all my right resign,
Entirely easy had they not been mine ;
Yet this reflection consolates my fate,
I see my error e'er it proves too late.

No more half maz'd I hurry thro' the town,
With magazines of projects in my crown,
While pyrate printers rob me of my gain,
And reap the labour'd harvest of my brain.

Like other men I walk a common pace,
Nor run thro' London one continu'd race ;
But know when, where, and what I am to do ;
You'll think it strange, my Lord, but yet 'tis true.

Thrice welcome, sweet tranquillity of mind !
I now a measure in contentment find ;
Can labour or relax whene'er I please,
And boast I've once enjoy'd a moment's ease ;
Of all a mod'rate man can wish possest,
But most in such a godlike patron blest,
Beneath the sacred sanction of whose name,
I build my present peace, my future fame.

A SORROWFUL LAMENTATION FOR THE LOSS OF A MAN AND NO MAN

In the Simple Style

As musing I rang'd in the meads all alone,
A beautiful creature was making her moan ;
O, the tears they did trickle full fast from her eyes,
And she pierced both the air and my heart with her
        cries.

I gently requested the cause of her moan ;
She told me her lov'd Senesino was flown ;
And in that sad posture she'd ever remain
Unless the dear creature would come back again.

Why, who is this mortal so cruel, said I,
That draws such a stream from so lovely an eye ?
He must be a base and a false-hearted man.
This fann'd but her sorrow, and thus she began.

'Tis neither for man nor for woman, said she,
That thus with lamenting I water the lee ;
But 'tis for a singer so charming and sweet,
Whose musick, Alas ! I shall never forget.

Perhaps 'tis some linnet or blackbird, said I,
Perhaps 'tis your skylark has ta'en to the sky
Come, dry up your tears and abandon your grief ;
Another I'll get but I'll give you relief.

No linnet, no blackbird, no skylark, said she,
But one who is better by far than all three ;
My dear Senesino, for whom thus I cry,
Is sweeter than all the wing'd songsters that fly.

Perhaps, pretty creature, your parrot is flown,
Your monkey, your lapdog occasions your moan ?
To all my surmises she answer'd me No,
And sobbed out eternally Se-ne-si-noh.

For Heaven's sake, dear creature, your sorrows unfold ;
To ease you I'll spare not for silver or gold.
But still she replied Ah ! Alas ! 'tis in vain ;
Nor silver nor gold can recall him again.

A curse upon silver, a curse upon gold,
That could not my dear Senesino withold ;
'Twas gold that first tempted him over the main ;
'Tis gold has transported him thither again.

Adieu to Faustina, Cuzzoni likewise,
Whom parties of courtiers extol to the skies ;
Adieu to the op'ra, adieu to the ball !
My darling is gone, and a fig for them all.

THE BEAU'S LAMENTATION FOR THE LOSS
OF FARRINELLI[1]

As saunt'ring I rang'd in the park all alone
A sparkish young fellow was making his moan ;
Oh, he cried like a child that had newly been whipp'd,
And vow'd he had rather at hazard been stripp'd,
For his dear Farrinelli had flown into Spain,
And he never should hear the sweet creature again.

Come, never lament for a singer, said I,
Can't English performers his absence supply ?
There's Beard,[2] and there's Salway,[2] and smart Kitty
    Clive,[3]
The pleasantest, merriest mortal alive.
Let's go to *The Dragon*,[4] good company's there,
There's Marg'ry and Mauxy and Signor Laguerre.

Oh, talk not of horrible English, said he,
I tell you Italian's the language for me.
'Tis better than Latin, 'tis better than Greek,
'Tis what all our nobles and gentry should speak ;
Plain English may serve for the cit or the clown,
But not at the elegant end of the town.

Fly, Heidegger,[5] fly, and my idol restore ;
O, let me but hear the enchanter once more,
For Handel may study, and study in vain
While Strada's[6] expell'd, and my Broschi's in Spain.
For Oh, his sweet warble so highly I prize,
Give him to my ears, I'll surrender my eyes.

A curse upon silver, a curse upon gold,
That could not my favourite songster withhold ;
'Tis gold that has tempted him over to Spain,
'Tis nothing but gold can allure him again.

Let's pay the sev'n hundred, and sev'n hundred more,
Nay, sev'n times sev'n thousand, and ten times ten
  score.

Adieu, Casserelli, Chimenti likewise,
Whom parties at Hickford's[7] extol to the skies ;
Adieu, Covent Garden, adieu, Drury Lane,
I never will darken a playhouse again.
Without Farrinelli the Op'ra must fall,
So I'll fling up my ticket, and not pay the call.

THE EFFEMINATE

Tell me, gentle hobby de hoy,
Art thou girl, or art thou boy ?
For thy features and thy dress
Such contraries do express.
I stand amaz'd, and at a loss to know
To what new species thou thy form dost owe.

By thy hair tuck'd up behind
Thou should'st be of womankind ;
Yet no woman thou can'st be,
For no petticoats we see.
Then to what sex, Alas ! hast thou a claim,
Who'rt either, neither, yet to both a shame.

If thou art a man, forbear
Thus this motley garb to wear ;
Let thy dress thy sex impart,
And appear like what thou art.
Like what thou art ! Oh no, pray pardon me ;
I mean appear like what you ought to be.

NAMBY-PAMBY

A Panegyric on the New Versification,
Address'd to A—— P——, Esq.[1]

Naughty Paughty Jack-a-Dandy,
Stole a Piece of Sugar Candy
From the Grocer's Shoppy-Shop,
And away did hoppy-hop.

All ye poets of the age,
All ye witlings of the stage,
Learn your jingles to reform,
Crop your numbers and conform.
Let your little verses flow
Gently, sweetly, row by row ;
Let the verse the subject fit,
Little subject, little wit.
Namby-Pamby is your guide,
Albion's joy, Hibernia's pride.
Namby-Pamby, pilly-piss,
Rhimy-pim'd on Missy Miss
Tartaretta Tartaree,
From the navel to the knee ;
That her father's gracy grace
Might give him a placy place.

He no longer writes of Mammy
Andromache[2] and her lammy,
Hanging-panging at the breast
Of a matron most distress'd.
Now the venal poet sings
Baby clouts and baby things,
Baby dolls and baby houses,
Little misses, little spouses,
Little playthings, little toys,
Little girls and little boys.

As an actor does his part,
So the nurses get by heart
Namby-Pamby's little rhimes,
Little jingle, little chimes,
To repeat to missy-miss,
Piddling ponds of pissy-piss ;
Cacking-packing like a lady,
Or bye-bying in the crady.
Namby-Pamby ne'er will die
While the nurse sings lullaby.
Namby-Pamby's doubly mild,
Once a man, and twice a child ;
To his hanging sleeves restor'd,
Now he foots it like a lord ;
Now he pumps his little wits,
Sh . . . ing writes, and writing sh . . . ts,
All by little tiny bits.
Now methinks I hear him say,
Boys and girls, come out to play !
Moon do's shine as bright as day.

Now my Namby-Pamby's found
Sitting on the friar's ground,
Picking silver, picking gold ;
Namby-Pamby's never old.
Bally-cally, they begin,
Namby-Pamby still keeps in.
Namby-Pamby is no clown.
London Bridge is broken down :
Now he courts the gay ladee,
Dancing o'er the Lady-Lee.
Now he sings of Lick-spit Lyar,
Burning in the brimstone fire ;
Lyar, lyar ! Lick-spit, Lick,
Turn about the candle stick !
Now he sings of Jacky Horner,
Sitting in the chimney corner,

8

Eating of a Christmas pye,
Putting in his thumb, O fie !
Putting in, O fie ! his thumb,
Pulling out, O strange, a plum.
Now he plays at Stee-Staw-Stud,
Sticking apples in the mud ;
When 'tis turn'd to Stee-Staw-Stire,
Then he sticks 'em in the mire.
Now he acts the grenadier,
Calling for a pot of beer.
Where's his money ?   He's forgot ;
Get him gone, a drunken sot.
Now a cock-horse does he ride,
And anon on timber stride.
See and Saw, and Sacch'ry Down,
London is a gallant town !
Now he gathers riches in,
Thicker, faster, pin by pin ;
Pins apiece to see his show,
Boys and girls flock row by row ;
From their clothes the pins they take,
Risk a whipping for his sake ;
From their cloaths the pins they pull
To fill Namby's cushion full.
So much wit at such an age
Does a genius great presage ;
Second childhood gone and past,
Should he prove a man at last,
What must second manhood be
In a child so bright as he.

   Guard him, ye poetic pow'rs,
Watch his minutes, watch his hours ;
Let your tuneful nine inspire him.
Let poetic fury fire him ;
Let the poets, one and all,
To his genius victims fall.

A NEW YEAR'S ODE FOR 1736-1737

Composed in a Dream, the Author imagining himself
to be the Poet Laureate[1]

A New Year's Ode ! Heav'ns ! how shall I begin ?
One year's gone, and t'other's just come in.
But yesterday, if I aright remember,
Was styl'd the one and thirtieth of December.
This present is the first of January.
Good lack a day !   How times and seasons vary !
'Tis an old subject, quite to tatters wore.
What can I say that ha'n't been said before ?
But I wish chronologers would fix
Whether 'tis thirty seven or thirty six.

THE HAPPY BEGGARS[1]

Tho' begging is an honest trade
Which wealthy knaves despise,
Yet rich men may be beggars made,
And we that beg may rise ;
The greatest kings may be betray'd
And lose their sov'reign power,
But he that stoops to ask his bread
Can never fall much lower.

Tho' foreigners have swarm'd of late
And spoil'd our begging trade,
Yet still we live and drink good beer,
Tho' they our rights invade ;
Some say they for religion fled,
But wiser people tell
That they were forc'd to leave their home
Because they would rebel.

Let heavy taxes greater grow
To make our army fight ;
Where 'tis not to be had, you know,
The king must lose his right ;
Let one side laugh, the other mourn,
We've no anxiety
But great lords will beggars be
To be as great as we.

What tho' we make the world believe
That we are sick or lame ?
'Tis now a virtue to deceive ;
Our teachers do the same.
In trade dissembling is no crime,
And we may live to see
That begging in a little time
The only trade will be.

THE TRUE TARR

A knave's a knave, tho' ne'er so brave,
Tho' diamonds round him shine ;
What tho' he's great, takes mighty state,
And thinks himself divine ;
His ill-got wealth can't give him health,
Or future ill prevent.
An honest tarr is richer far
If he enjoys content.

A soul sincere scorns fraud or fear,
Within itself secure.
For vice will blast, but virtue last
While truth and time endure.
Blow high, blow low, from fate or foe
He scorns to tack about.
But to his trust is strictly just,
And nobly stems it out.

THE PRUDE

The squeamish prude
Will say you're rude
If you speak but a word amiss ;
And yet in the dark
With her fav'rite spark
Most eagerly she'll kiss.

The Drury crew
She'll far outdo
When she throws off all restraint ;
Yet in publick so precise
Is this devil in disguise,
You'd take her for a saint.

THE PRUDE DEMOLISH'D

SHE :   I will not bear it,
         I do declare it ;
         I will call out if you're so rude.
HE :   Madam, I know it,
         Your looks they show it ;
         I plainly see that you're a prude.

SHE :   A prude, what then, sir ?
         I scorn such men, sir ;
         Pray leave me to myself alone.
HE :   Sweet, pretty creature,
         Compose that feature ;
         Prudes ne'er cry out but when they're blown.

THE FORTUNE-HUNTER'S MENTAL
RESERVATION

Madam, your eyes (or diamonds) shine so bright,
I'm captivated by the dazzling sight :
You have ten thousand charms (pounds I should say) ;
Those eyes (or bags) have stol'n my heart away.
In pity, then, some comfort to me give,
Pay all my debts, and keep me while I live.

THE POWER OF GOLD

The fair are soonest pierc'd with golden darts ;
The king of diamonds is their king of hearts.
Where merit fails, there money does bewitch,
For 'tis sufficient merit to be rich.
Beauty was purchas'd by desert of old,
But now, Alas ! 'tis bought with sordid gold.

THE MODERATOR BETWEEN THE
FREEMASONS AND THE GORMOGONS[1]

The Masons and the Gormogons
Are laughing at one another,
While all mankind are laughing at them ;
Then why do they make such a pother ?

They bait their hooks for simple gulls,
And truth with bam they smother ;
But when they've taken in their culls,
Why, then 'tis . . . *Welcome, Brother.*

AN EXTEMPORE THOUGHT ON FLATTERY

Flatt'ry's a base, unmanly, coward vice,
A lurking devil in a fair disguise.
A real friend will all our faults reprove,
And mix with outward anger inward love ;
But flatt'rers kill with a more private blow,
And outward love for inward hatred show.

DEMOCRITUS LAUGHING AT THE FOLLY
OF FLATTERY

Ha ! Ha ! Ha ! Ha ! . . . hold me or I shall burst ;
Could anyone have thought the fellow durst
Abuse a fool so grossly to his face,
Or think to flatter with so ill a grace.

Sir, said the slave, to speak your worth,
Or set your eminent perfections forth,
Some more than common genius does require,
Blest with a Cato or a Virgil's fire ;
Yet what I cannot praise, permit me to admire.

Heavens ! What a shape is there, how nicely turn'd !
A face, too, how with ev'ry grace adorn'd !
And Heaven, to make its fairest work complete,
Has to those beauties join'd a soul as great.

This is not half, but when he'd made an end
The flatter'd fool embrac'd him, call'd him friend,
Wish'd for an opportunity to show
How much he for so dear a friend could do.

Sir, said the sycophant, there is a place
Now vacant, which I gladly would embrace ;
Your business, answer'd t'other, shall be done ;
This moment I'll to court about it run.
He fled with eager joy ; when I approach'd,
And on the flatt'rer's company encroach'd.
I ask'd him who he was that he so prais'd.
Said he, A wicked villain, who has rais'd
Himself by fraud, by perjury, and all
That we can odious, black, or vicious call.

Amaz'd, I left the monster as I would
Infected persons, or contagious blood.
Such unexpected baseness chang'd my note,
And stopp'd the rising laughter in my throat.
I could have wept ; but why do I exclaim ?
Mankind, alas, will ever be to blame.
The world will still its vicious courses keep ;
Let doting Heraclitus wail and weep ;
But while such shoals of fools and knaves there be,
There's store enough of laughter still for me.

MRS. STUART'S RETIREMENT

From the court to the cottage convey me away,
For I'm weary of grandeur and what they call gay,
   Where pride without measure,
   And pomp without pleasure
Makes life in a circle of hurry decay.

Far remote and retir'd from the noise of the town,
I'll exchange my brocade for a plain russet gown.
   My friends shall be few,
   But well chosen and true,
And sweet recreation our evening shall crown.

With a rural repast, a rich banquet to me,
On a mossy green bank near some shady old tree,
   The river's clear brink
   Shall afford me my drink,
And temp'rance my friendly physician shall be.

Ever calm and serene, with contentment still blest,
Not too giddy with joy, or with sorrow deprest ;
   I'll neither invoke
   Nor repine at death's stroke,
But retire from the world as I would to my rest.

THE RETIREMENT

A Satire

Adieu to all the follies of the town,
Where noise and hurry all enjoyment drown,
Where vice o'er virtue has pre-eminence,
And nonsense gets the upper hand of sense
Where honesty and honour are oppress'd ;
Where but the name of virtue is profess'd,
While virtue's self is grown a very jest.

There fops in state and pomp securely ride,
And view the crowd beneath with scorn and pride ;
Or born to riches, or the fools of fate,
They know no virtue but a good estate.
To them the wise and good must humbly bow,
And meet, perhaps, a stern and scornful brow ;
While pandars, knaves, and parasites more bold
Fawn at their feet, and fleece them of their gold.

There all things borrow'd shapes and dresses wear,
And no-one's really what he would appear.
Merit is laugh'd at, modesty despis'd,
The knave and wealthy fool alike are priz'd.
Contempt and pride on ev'ry face is seen,
And hatred lurks beneath the formal grin.

They'll wound their dearest friends in sport and play
For reputation is their darling prey.
Nor can they bear to see another rise,
But look on merit with invidious eyes ;
For be an action ne'er so just or good,
'Tis soon misconstru'd and misunderstood.
The sly objection and malicious sneer
Can make a worthy soul a fiend appear.

And yet so double are their tongues and hearts,
That while they wound you with their sland'rous darts,
If you perchance appear they seem to fly,
And meet you in a treach'rous ecstasy ;
Embrace you in their false, deceitful arms,
While ev'n your faults are now transform'd to charms.
You simply take the flatt'rers for your friends,
And wish and study how to make amends :
But the same moment that your back is turn'd,
Again you're laugh'd at, and again you're scorn'd.

Here, let me, then, forget the noisy town,
My rest of life with solid pleasures crown.
Kind nature here does joys untainted yield
In ev'ry grove, in ev'ry flow'ry field.
A thousand various sweets she does present,
To bless the mind with undisturb'd content.
In these blest shades for ever let me stay,
While the soft moments gently glide away.
No care, no tumult shall my peace molest ;
Storms may disturb the world, but not my rest.

THE TOWN SPARK AND THE COUNTRY LASS

Come, come, my dear nymph, now all nature looks gay,
Now birds sweetly whistle, and lambs sweetly play,
To yonder cool shade let us quickly retire,
And taste all the pleasures that love can inspire.

Good sir, not so hasty.   We innocent maids
Too oft are deceiv'd by you arch London blades ;
How many poor damsels deluded by you
Are forc'd ever after their folly to rue.

O, think not, my fairest, so meanly of me ;
No harm, on my honour, shall happen to thee.
Here's gold that buys all things, and silver good store,
And when that is gone I'll supply thee with more.

I'll trust not your honour, your gold I despise ;
My virtue above all temptations I prize ;
Tho' poor I am honest ; I'm not to be sold,
So pray take away both yourself and your gold.

I'll take thee to London, and deck thee so fine
That thou shalt the greatest of ladies outshine,
And ride in a coach to the park and the play,
All glitt'ring with diamonds, outsparkling the day.

No, sir, I abhor such a scandalous life ;
I'll be no mortal's miss, but some honest man's wife ;
So pray, sir, return to the place whence you came,
For I'll ne'er buy my pride at the price of my fame.

I love thee so dearly, I'll not be deny'd.
Thy virtue so charms me, I'll make thee my bride.
Then come, my dear angel, in wedlock let's join,
I long till I make thee eternally mine.

Then, sir, I assure you your love shan't be lost ;
What I want in my portion I'll spare in my cost ;
Your int'rest, your pleasure I'll closely attend,
And save many pounds which your London wives
    spend.

I'll drink not, I'll game not, I'll wear no fine cloaths,
To squander your wealth, and decoy the town beaux ;
But love you for ever, and prove all my life
A constant, affectionate, dutiful wife.

I hasten, I hasten to fill thy fond arms ;
No wealth, no possessions can equal thy charms ;
Let libertines live to repent, while we prove
No pleasure so lasting as virtuous love.

SALLY SWEETBREAD

Now the good man's from home
I could cast away care,
And with some brisk fellow
Steal out to the fair ;
But some are too bashful,
And some are too bold,
And woman's intentions
Are not to be told.

But could I once meet
With a spark to my mind,
One fit to be trusted,
I then might prove kind ;
With him I'd steal out,
And I'd range the fair round,
Both eating and drinking
The best could be found.

125

Oh ! there I shall see
The fine gentleman rakes,
And hear the sweet cry
Of beer, ale, wine, and cakes ;
While I in blue apron
And clean linen gown
Allure all the sparks
From the flirts of the town.

There's Fielding[1] and Oates[1]
There's Hippesley[2] and Hall,[1]
There's Pinchbeck[3] and Fawkes,[4]
There's the devil and all.
I'll have the best place
And I'll see ev'ry sight,
And revel in pleasure
From morning to night.

Then home get secure
E'er my husband comes back ;
And cry most demurely,
What d'ye buy, what d'ye lack ;
Thus courted and treated,
Gallanted and kiss'd,
Can deary be cheated
When nothing is miss'd.

THE HAPPY BUTCHERS' WIVES

O, the apron we carry before us,
This plentiful till
Commands what we will.
It makes ev'ry mortal adore us,
So happy are butchers' wives.

To keep out the cold in the morning,
We've always a pot
Of something's that hot,
Our husbands to hinder us scorning,
So happy are butchers' wives.

At noon, wherever we dine, too,
We eat of the best
Which nicely is dress'd ;
Nor want we our share of good wine, too,
So happy are butchers' wives.

All night at each other's houses,
With a supper and song
When evenings are long,
We regale with our neighbours and spouses,
So happy are butchers' wives.

Then home to rest retiring,
The curtain's drawn
Till morning's slow dawn.
There needs no great enquiring
How happy are butchers' wives !

THE CONTENTED CUCKOLD

A cuckold, it is thought a most reproachful name.
Tho' wives commit the fault, yet husbands bear the
　　blame ;
'Tis easy for a woman a little slip to make,
And if it were uncommon, how many heads would
　　ache ?

I'll give my wife her humour if she but give me mine,
And if I feel a tumour I never shall repine :
If she a cuckold make me, I'll pay her in her kind,
And may the devil take me if e'er I lag behind.

THE BEAU MONDE,

OR

THE PLEASURES OF ST. JAMES'

A Ballad to the Tune of " Oh, London is a Fine Town "

Oh, St. James' is a lovely place,
　　'Tis better than the city ;
For there are balls and operas,
　　And everything that's pretty.

There's little Lady Cuzzoni,
　　And fisking Dame Faustina ;
The deuce a bit will either sing
　　Unless they're each a queen-a.

And when we've eek'd out history,
　　And made them rival queens,
They'll warble sweetly on the stage,
　　And scold behind the scenes ;

When, having fill'd their pockets full,
   No longer can they stay,
But turn their backs upon the town,
   And scamper all away.

The belles and beaux cry after them
   With all their might and main ;
And Heidegger is sent in haste
   To fetch 'em back again.

Then hey for a subscription
   To th'opera or ball ;
The silver ticket wags about
   Until there comes a call.

This puts them into doleful dumps
   Who were both blithe and gay ;
There's nothing spoils diversion more
   Than telling what's to pay.

Oh, there's Miss Polly Peachum hugs
   Our nobles by the ears,
Till Ponder Well by far exceeds
   The musick of the spheres.

Who, Lo ! to show the wisdom great
   Of London's famous town,
We set her up above herself,
   And then we take her down.

And there's your beaux, with powder'd cloaths,
   Bedaub'd from head to shin :
Their pocket-holes adorn'd with gold,
   But not a souse within.

And there's your pretty gentlemen,
   All dress'd in silk and satin,
That get a piece of ev'rything,
   Excepting sense and Latin.

Who brag and bounce till danger comes,
   Oh ! then they lag and falter,
And think it better to resign
   Than venture to Gibraltar.

And there's your cits that have their tits
   In Finsbury so sweet,
But costlier tits they keep, God wot,
   In Bond and Poultney Street.

And there's your green nobility,
   On citizens so witty,
Whose fortunes and gentility
   Arose from London's city.

Our fathers labour'd for our ease,
   And left us store of treasure ;
Then let us make the most of life,
   And lay it out in pleasure.

We go to bed when others rise,
   And dine at candle-light ;
There's nothing mends complexion more
   Than turning day to night.

For what is title, wealth, or wit,
   If folks are not genteel ?
Oh, how can they be said to live
   Who know not what's quadrille ?

POLLY PEACHUM

Of all the toasts that Britain boasts,
   The gim, the gent, the jolly,
The brave, the fair, the debonair,
   There's none cry'd up like Polly ;
She's fir'd the town, has quite cut down
   The opera of Rolli ;[1]
Go where you will, the subject still
   Is pretty, pretty Polly.

There's Madam Faustina, Catso !
   And eek Madam Cuzzoni ;
Likewise Signor Senesino
   Are *tutti Abbandonni* :
Ha, Ha, Ha, Ha, Do, Re, Mi, Fa,
   Are now but farce and folly ;
We're ravish'd all with Toll, Loll, Loll,
   And pretty, pretty Polly.

The sons of Bayes in lyric lays
   Sound forth their names in print-o ;
And as we pass, in frame and glass
   We see her mezzotint-o.
In Ivy Lane the city strain
   Is now no more on Dolly,
And all the brights at Man's and White's[2]
   Of nothing talk but Polly.

Ah ! Johnny Gay, thy lucky play
   Has made the critics grin-a ;
They cry 'tis flat, 'tis this, 'tis that,
   But let them laugh that win-a ;
I swear parbleu, 'tis naif and new,
   Ill nature is but folly ;
'Thas lent a stitch to rent of Rich,[3]
   And set up Madam Polly.

131

Ah, tuneful fair, beware, beware,
  Nor toy with star and garter ;
Fine cloaths may hide a foul inside,
  And you may catch a tartar.
If powder'd fop blow up your shop
  'Twill make you melancholy ;
Then, left to rot, you'll die forgot.
  Alas, Alas ! poor Polly.

POLLY'S BIRTHDAY

'Tis wond'rous hard
A licensed bard
Can only now be witty,
Or dare rehearse
In hide bound verse
His lamentable ditty.
So I'll not sing
Of George our King,
But of angelick Polly.
'Tis her birthday,
Let all be gay,
Let ev'ry soul be jolly.

Within her face
Shines ev'ry grace
Can give beholders pleasure.
Her heav'n born mind
Is most refin'd,
'Tis truth and virtue's treasure.
Of all approv'd,
By all belov'd,
Most noble is her spirit ;
So he's an ass
That baulks his glass
To so much worth and merit.

MORNING CRIES

How contented on the plain
Is the happy shepherd swain !
His peaceful breast
Is quite at rest,
No cares perplex his brain.
How much unlike the courtly rake,
Who dates his night from morning's break.
Tho' e'er so much his head does ache
No rest, no quietness can he take
While Sweep, Sweep, Sweep ! Old lead or old brass !
Take money for your old flint glass !
Knives to grind ! Knives, scissors, penknives to grind !
Old cloaks, suits or coats ! Any work for the cooper !
Come buy my card matches, come buy them of me,
For they be the best matches as ever you see.
Dust Ho ! Any milk ! Sweep, Sweep !
Disturbs his sleep, and keeps him half awake.

How contented on the grass
Sits the happy country lass,
While all the day
Her lambkins play ;
How sweet the moments pass !
How much unlike the courtly dame,
Just come from masquerade or game,
That e'er so much her head does ache,
No rest, no quiet can she take,
While Sweep, Sweep, Sweep ! Old lead or old brass !
Take money for your old flint glass !
Knives to grind ! Knives, scissors, penknives to grind !
Old cloaks, suits or coats ! Any work for the cooper !
Come buy my card matches, come buy them of me,
For they be the best matches as ever you see.
Dust Ho ! Any milk ! Sweep, Sweep !
Disturbs her sleep, and keeps her half awake.

133

THE SURLY PEASANT

Let whimsical monarchs of state
Imagine themselves to be great;
With my spade in my hand
Sole monarch I stand
Of twenty good acres of land.

A fig for your sir or your madam;
Our origin all is from Adam;
Then why should I buckle,
Palaver or truckle
To any pragmatical chuckle?

THE DISPARITY OF YOUTH AND AGE

What should a merry, airy, lively, youthful, blooming
    lass
Do with a mumbling, bumbling, grumbling, stumbling,
    fumbling ass?
Youth and age but ill agree.
Such a man's no match for me;
Coughing, spitting,
Thwarting, twitting,
Ever teasing,
Never pleasing;
Hang his money, hang his bags,
Give me youth, content and rags.

THE EFFECTS OF GAMING

A curse on cards, a curse on dice,
A curse on gaming, cursed vice !
It wastes our time, it wastes our wealth,
And is the modish way of stealth.

Where gaming spreads its fatal gloom,
There mirth and music flee the room,
And rage and discord take their place,
And falsehood fleers in ev'ry face.

In pleasures men may be profuse,
And for each failing find excuse,
But gaming has no other end
But ruin of yourself or friend.

THE ANTIQUATED COQUETTE

Viella, why at fifty nine,
Thus gay, thus brisk dost thou appear ?
Why do sparkling diamonds shine
In thy party-colour'd hair ?

Why art thou seen at balls and plays
In gaudy garments dress'd ?
You say whole crowds upon you gaze ;
I grant you . . . 'tis confess'd.

The youthful ridiculing train
With inward smiles behold
A wretch like you so very vain,
And yet so very old.

Yet thou can'st talk of warm desire,
And of the joys of love,
When thou art ready to expire,
And ought'st to look above.

For shame, Viella, cease to ape
The blooming, sprightly fair.
In gear of gauze, and weed of crape
You'd like yourself appear.

THE OLD BEAU

*Or a full and true Account of a certain Apothecary
that turn'd Gallant at Sixty Three*

Not far from London's wealthy town
   A doctor there doth dwell,
Who in the knowledge of close-stools
   All others does excel.

A man of mickle might is he,
   And wond'rous in his skill,
To make a med'cine for a horse,
   Or give a dog a pill.

What pity 'tis so wise a man
   Should feeble be and old ;
Nay, worse, that he should be in love,
   As I, for sooth ! am told.

But that so old a man should love
   Why need we to admire ?
For touchwood, when 'tis rotten grown,
   Is soonest set on fire.

And oft we see the aged horse,
   When he's of strength bereft,
Tho' all his teeth are gone but one
   He has a colt's tooth left.

Thus far'd it with our doctor dear ;
   O Cupid, 'twas unkind
To strike a dart at sixty three !
   But thou wert always blind.

O, had you seen this man in love
  You would have laugh'd good store ;
For sure since Adam such a wight
  Was never seen before.

With gaudy garb o'er wither'd limbs
  Our doctor did appear,
Much like an overgrown baboon,
  Dress'd up at Southwark Fair.

On old and young, both far and near
  His practice now he tries ;
And courts full forty at a time,
  For twenty won't suffice.

The ladies all blow up the fire,
  And swell the empty thing ;
They let him prate his bellyfull,
  For he has lost his sting.

Haste, emp'rick, haste thee to thy drugs,
  Go seek a med'cine there
That may extinguish this fierce flame
  E'er midsummer draw near.

Give o'er for shame, 'tis now high time
  To think on thy condition.
Go fit thyself for t'other world,
  And be thy own physician.

A STORY OF A COCK AND A BULL

Multorum Manibus Grande Levatur Onus

In Italy not long ago
There was a governor, you know,
Who in short space, as we are told,
Fill'd all his bags with store of gold.
The honest townsmen vext to see
Themselves become as poor . . . as me,
They were in such a wretched taking
It set their very hearts a-aching ;
And therefore, to remove this dudgeon,
They were resolv'd the old curmudgeon
Without a further noise or rout
Should leave the city and turn out.
But while this mighty resolution
Waited for thanks and execution,
Up starts a fellow with a beard,
Whom ev'rybody lov'd and fear'd.
Hearkee, good folks, said he, I pray ;
D'ye know what 'tis you mean ; you say
We'd turn the governor away ;
But hold, without much farther arguing,
There want two words to make the bargain.
'Tis true, you say that trading's dull,
And that the governor's bags are full,
So very full they all run o'er ;
Why, then, ye fools, they'll hold no more ;
But if another man should come
In Mr. What-d'ye-call-him's room,
He'll bring a family in rags,
And whole cartloads of empty bags,
Which he will fill as how you know,
And, neighbours, pray what think ye now ?
At this the rabble shook their heads,
They cross'd themselves, and told their beads

To think a man so old as he
Into such deep affairs should see,
While he, to raise their admiration,
Tickl'd their ears with this relation.
A man there was, said he, whose field
Good store of glorious corn did yield,
Which to preserve a cock he set
To watch all hours, dry and wet ;
To be awake both night and morn,
That none might steal away the corn.
But e'er two days pass'd o'er his head
He came and saw the cock had fed
So heartily that he grew fat.
The thrifty hind, provok'd at that,
Sent Cock-a-Doodle waddling home,
And brought a brace of bulls in's room.
Then three days more at home he stay'd,
But when he came he was dismay'd :
Good Lord ! How he did storm and roar !
He now was madder than before.
Then did he stamp, and rave, and cry,
And made a noise, good reason why ;
The wanton bulls had made such haste
To lay the whole enclosure waste,
That as I live . . .
'Twixt Monday night and Friday morn
They had not left one ear of corn.

BLUNDRELLA,

OR

THE IMPERTINENT,

A Tale

The tea was drunk and ta'en away,
No soul had anything to say ;
The weather and the usual din
Were going to begin again ;
Fashion and scandal, drain'd before,
On carpet had been brought once more,
But for Blundrella, common pest
Of the polite, the standing jest.

Blundrella, idol of the vain,
And first in the loquacious train ;
In all things ignorant and weak,
Yet on all subjects would she speak ;
And of her own perfections vaunted,
Still daunting all, but never daunted ;
Of the most contradicting spirit,
And envious of another's merit.
This creature thus with saucy air
Address'd Belinda, blooming fair.

Madam, I'm told you sing. I long
To have the honour of a song :
Much better bred than to refuse,
Belinda pleads the old excuse :
She's caught a cold, and feigns a cough,
But that, alas, won't bring her off ;
Blundrella urges the request,
Now seconded by all the rest.

At length, unwilling to appear
Affected, peevish, or severe,
The lovely virgin tun'd her voice,
More out of complaisance than choice,
While all were with her musick pleas'd
But she who had the charmer teas'd,
Who, rude, unmanner'd and abrupt,
Did thus Belinda interrupt.

Madam, said the affected thing,
Did you ne'er hear Squallinda sing?
I've heard her sing that very song
Would charm the whole seraphick throng;
Of all the singers, her for me,
She sings so sweet, so clear, so free.
But, madam, can't you sing another?
That song, I hope, has got a brother.
Let us have that which the Faustina
Sings when she hangs on Senesino.
Its name I have forgot; no matter;
'Tis that which makes the boxes clatter.
Or, madam! . . . but I beg your pardon
There is a song that in the garden
Cuzzoni sings unto her son.
That or another, all is one.

Belinda blush'd with shame and rage;
But yet, unwilling to engage
So bold a foe in such a fray,
She let the creature have her way;
And tho' at sight she sang her part,
And was a mistress of the art,
Pleaded her want of voice and skill,
Which made Blundrella prouder still,
Who grew insufferably vain,
And alter'd both her voice and strain.

She talk'd of singers and composers,
Of their admirers and opposers,
Of the Cuzzoni and Faustini,
Of Handel, and of Bononcini ;
One was too rough, t'other too smooth ;
Atillio only hit her tooth,
And *Tamo Tanto* was a song
Would give her pleasure all day long.

Full loftily she gave her vote ;
This had no voice, and that no throat ;
Heidegger had receiv'd a letter,
And we should shortly have a better :
A messenger was sent to Dover
To wait the lady's coming over,
Who should no sooner hither come
But she would strike all others dumb.

She likewise grew exceeding witty
Upon the concerts of the city.
'Tis true, she lik'd the Castle best,
And yet she made 'em both a jest.
Nor did she much admire the Crown,
But as 'twas t'other end of town.

She next of masters gan to preach ;
The English were not fit to teach ;
Italians were the only men,
And ev'n of those not one in ten,
For she had heard a lady say
Scarce two in town could sing or play.

What with composers, players, singers,
Performance, gusto, voices, fingers,
She ran herself quite out of breath,
And talk'd the company to death.

When haply, with engaging air,
Eugenio, darling of the fair,
Who touches charmingly the flute,
Enter'd, and struck Blundrella mute,
And kept her clack eternal under
For near a minute. There's a wonder!
Eugenio must expect his share,
For scarce had he assum'd a chair
But she, impatient, silence broke,
And running to him, thus she spoke.

Now for a tune, my pretty man!
Nay, you shall play, say what you can;
Ladies, he's the delightful'st creature
You ever knew. No soul plays sweeter.
Nay, prithee now, don't make a rout;
Here 'tis, egad, come, pull it out.

What mortal man could stand the trial?
He must consent, there's no denial.
So for mere quiet sake he plays,
While she e'en stifles him with praise,
And worries the poor man to death,
Nor suffers him to take his breath,
But calls for tune on tune so fast
Eugenio is quite tir'd at last,
And begs a truce upon parole;
He'll play anon with all his soul.

Now you must know Belinda's charms
Had giv'n this spark no small alarms;
He was her servant most avow'd,
And happiest of the sighing crowd.
Saphronia, being her near relation,
Haply laid hold on this cessation,

And to Eugenio drawing near
She whisper'd softly in his ear,
Told him Blundrella's vile assurance,
And sweet Belinda's mild endurance.

Eugenio instantly was fir'd,
Rage and revenge his mind inspir'd :
He re-assum'd his speech and flute,
And thus Blundrella did salute.
Madam, said he, before I go
Your dear commands I'd gladly know.

Blundrella rear'd her crest aloft,
And begg'd him to play something soft.
What think you, madam, of *Al Ombra*?
But that's too old ; d'ye like *Sgombra*?
Si Caro, if you please, said she ;
He play'd the tune of *Children Three*.
She was in raptures, and entreated
The self same tune might be repeated.

He chang'd his airs, and to her shame
She took ten others for the same.
In short, Eugenio play'd her off,
And made her all the circle's scoff :
While stupid, she ascrib'd to wit and sense
The laughter rais'd by her impertinence.

THE BALLAD OF KING JOHN'S SON AND THE CYNDER WENCH

To the Tune of " Chevy Chase "

When as King John did rule this land
  He had an only son,
No more like to his own papa
  Than an apple is like a gun.

Which prince, upon a May morning,
  Was sitting on a bench,
And there he chanc'd to fall in love
  With a dirty cynder wench.

Her hands and face were all begrim'd,
  And dirty was her skin ;
Her cloaths were nasty, torn, and old,
  And all not worth a pin.

Her hair was clotted to her head,
  Her nose it stood awry,
And eek her large, blue eyes, God wot,
  Did squint most damnably.

Her teeth were rotten in her gums,
  Her mouth it was so wide
That, as I live, a coach and six
  Within the same might ride.

Her back was hump'd, her breasts like dugs
  Did hang her waste adown,
And there commodiously display'd
  A skin of wainscot brown.

But, ladies fair, I will no more
  This ugly tale pursue,
Lest I should make your hearts full sick,
  And turn your stomachs too.

Yet Ah! Alas! and Well-a-Day!
  'Twere pity great, I wis,
A prince so nobly born should love
  So foul a drab as this.

But love does overcome the wise,
  The foolish eek withal,
The young, the old, the rich, the poor,
  The great as well as small.

So far'd it with our noble prince;
  His love he couldn't conceal,
But thus unto the cynder wench
  The same he did reveal.

Thou paragon of beauty bright,
  Thou most illustrious dame,
Since I was born my eyes ne'er saw
  So exquisite a frame.

Peerless thou art, thine eyes they shine
  Like some enliv'ning ray
Which Phoebus darts from out the sky
  To gild the dawn of day.

In ev'ry feature of thy face
  A thousand charms unite
To captivate our willing hearts,
  And bless our wond'rous sight.

147

The lily white, the blushing rose,
  Within thy cheeks combine ;
Their lively tinctures blended make
  Thy beauties more divine.

The coral equals not thy lips,
  Thy teeth in order show
Like bars of polish'd ivory,
  Adjusted, row by row.

Like two fair hills of alpine snow
  Thy downy breasts appear,
Thy neck as alabaster smooth,
  But much more white and clear.

Thy face, thy stature, and thy make,
  Thy air and thy address,
Are far beyond the pow'r of verse
  Or prose for to express.

Nor do thy beauties crave for ought
  Which might the same adorn ;
Thy costly robes, so richly deck'd,
  Bespeak thee nobly born.

Grant me thy love, O princess fair !
  For I adore thee so,
That as you love or hate, so I
  Possess or weal or woe.

While thus upon his bended knees
  This noble prince implor'd,
His words were met with looks of scorn
  From her whom he ador'd.

I mar'l, thou royster rude, quoth she,
   What makes thee taunt me so ;
I ne'er was so miscall'd before,
   I'd have thee for to know.

Full twenty husbands I have had,
   All men of mickle might ;
And dost thou think I'd stoop so low
   To lig by such a wight.

Go, get thee gone, Sir Knave, quoth she ;
   With that, upon his ear
She gave him such a swinging box
   As made him for to rear.

I should have said to reel, but that
   Would not have been a rhime ;
One word for think and one for sense
   Is good at any time.

This box did so alarm the prince,
   He straightway on her gaz'd ;
But when he saw her ugliness,
   Good Lord ! he was amaz'd.

Fly, hated object, then said he,
   Let me not see thy face ;
Thine hideous form I now perceive
   With horror and disgrace.

And for that box she gave the prince,
   He gave her kicks full twain,
And vow'd that he would never love
   A cynder wench again.

*Here followeth a right witty application, pithy, and well
applied to the whole*

You British ladies who have heard
   This most enchanting song,
Mark well the application
   Does unto you belong.

Your beauties only are divine
   While you have lovers score ;
But when adorers they grow scant,
   Your charms are then no more.

It is the eyes of pore-blind love
   Which makes you past compare ;
When with indifference we look,
   You are but as you were.

Then to your lovers all be kind,
   Be kind e'er 'tis too late ;
Lest, when the charms decay, you find
   The cynder wench's fate.

THE BALLAD OF SALLY IN OUR ALLEY

The Argument

A vulgar error having long prevail'd among many persons, who imagine Sally Salisbury the subject of this ballad, the author begs leave to undeceive and assure them it has not the least allusion to her, he being a stranger to her very name at the time this song was compos'd. For as innocence and virtue were ever the boundaries of his muse, so in this little poem he had no other view than to set forth the beauty of a chaste and disinterested passion, even in the lowest class of human life. The real occasion was this: A shoemaker's 'prentice, making holiday with his sweetheart, treated her with a sight of Bedlam, the puppet-shews, the flying chairs, and all the elegancies of Moorfields, from whence proceeding to the farthing pye-house, he gave her a collation of buns, cheese-cakes, gammon of bacon, stuff'd beef, and bottl'd ale, through all which scenes the author dodg'd them, charm'd with the simplicity of their court-ship, from which he drew this little sketch of nature ; but being then young and obscure, he was very much ridicul'd by some of his acquaintance for this performance, which, nevertheless, made its way into the polite world, and amply recompensed him by the applause of the divine Addison, who was pleased more than once to mention it with approbation.

Of all the girls that are so smart
　　There's none like pretty Sally ;
She is the darling of my heart,
　　And she lives in our alley.

There's ne'er a lady in the land
　　That's half so sweet as Sally ;
She is the darling of my heart,
　　And she lives in our alley.

Her father he makes cabbage-nets,
　　And thro' the streets does cry 'em ;
Her mother she sells laces long
　　To such as please to buy 'em ;
But sure such folks could ne'er beget
　　So sweet a girl as Sally ;
She is the darling of my heart,
　　And she lives in our alley.

When she is by I leave my work,
　　I love her so sincerely ;
My master comes like any Turk
　　And bangs me most severely ;
But let him bang his bellyfull,
　　I'll bear it all for Sally ;
She is the darling of my heart,
　　And she lives in our alley.

Of all the days that's in the week
　　I dearly love but one day,
And that's the day that comes betwix
　　A Saturday and Monday,
For then I'm dressed all in my best
　　To walk abroad with Sally ;
She is the darling of my heart,
　　And she lives in our alley.

My master carries me to church,
　　And often am I blam'd
Because I leave him in the lurch
　　As soon as text is nam'd ;

I leave the church in sermon time
    And slink away to Sally ;
She is the darling of my heart,
    And she lives in our alley.

When Christmas comes about again,
    O, then I shall have money ;
I'll hoard it up, and box and all,
    I'll give it to my honey ;
And would it were ten thousand pounds,
    I'd give it all to Sally ;
She is the darling of my heart,
    And she lives in our alley.

My master and the neighbours all
    Make game of me and Sally,
And, but for her, I'd better be
    A slave, and row a galley ;
But when my seven long years are out,
    O, then I'll marry Sally ;
O, then we'll wed, and then we'll bed,
    But not in our alley.

THE TRAGICAL STORY OF A MARE

A Burlesque Cantata

Unhappy me, what shall I do ?
My poor, dear mare has lost her shoe,
And I've no money to buy her new.
Some drunken rascal in the night
Has torn her saddle out of spite ;
'Thas ruin'd and undone me quite.

But what does most my soul assail
Is that, in fury of his ale,
The cursed sot has lopp'd her tail.

Aria Affettuosa

Oh mare, Oh mare, well may'st thou grumble ;
Thy shoe is lost, and thou must stumble.
Surely the fellow's brains were addle
That cropp'd thy tail, and tore thy saddle.

Da Capo

A WHIMSICAL DIALOGUE

Between the Author and his Favourite Mare,
Occasion'd by her Stumbling

MARE.   O master, I have lost my crupper.

MASTER. Then, mistress, you shall lose your supper.

MARE.   Nay, worse than that, I've broke my knees.

MASTER. Break your neck, madam, if you please.

MARE.   Then who must carry your gundy gut ?

MASTER. Why, I can walk, you saucy slut.

MARE.   I wish you would : what makes you ride,
And poor, unhappy me bestride ?
With such a weight you crush me down,
That as we pass from town to town
The people cry, Was ever seen
A man so fat, a mare so lean ?

MASTER. I prize the vulgar not a pin ;
'Tis not my fault that you're so thin.
Hadn't you enough of corn and hay,
At least three quarterns ev'ry day ?

MARE.   But then, dear sir, you work me so
That I can hardly stand or go ;
No rest from Saturday to Monday,
For, heathen-like, you ride on Sunday,
And lest one hour I should stand still,
I'm harrass'd by your brats and Will ;[1]
With two at once upon my back
I'm really made a perfect hack ;
I neither younger grow nor stronger ;
In short, I can hold out no longer.

My labour far exceeds my meat,
My shoes are batter'd off my feet ;
Nor will I carry . . .
. . . . a bard so odd
Unless I'm better fed and shod.

MASTER. Say what you will, we must contrive
Some way to see my daughter Clive.[2]

MARE. Why, there's the stage coach and the barge,
But you want me to save the charge.
Upon my soul ! you'd better stay,
For I shall drop you by the way.
Besides, you told me you could walk.

MASTER. Hussy ! d'ye know to whom you talk ?
I'll send you to the collar-maker's.

MARE. You'd better send me to twelve acres.
The worthiest man in all the nation
Has giv'n me there an invitation,
In Walthamstow's delightful mead
At liberty to range and feed ;
From labour free, and quite at ease,
To cull the herbage where I please.
There, if you would but let me stay
Until the latter end of May,
Take a walk down, and you shall see
The vast improvements made in me.
With skin so sleek and flowing mane,
You'll hardly know your mare again.
Then keep me only for your use,
Nor of good nature make abuse ;
But treat me gentler than before,
And I shall never stumble more.

PHOEBUS MISTAKEN,

OR

THE WAY TO CATCH A COY ONE

From the French

Turn, Daphne, turn ! Apollo said,
When he pursued the flying maid.
I am, said he, the god of verse ;
But Daphne still maintain'd her course.

Again he cry'd, Stop, stop, my dear !
With my lute I'll charm thy ear ;
She heard, 'tis true, but still she ran
Down the hills and o'er the plain.

At length she out of sight was flown,
And poor Apollo left alone.

Ah, Phoebus, hadst thou said, My dear,
Hither turn thee, cease to fear,
I am the god of cheerful day,
Youthful, handsome, sprightly, gay . . .
Those words alone the nymph had mov'd
She would have turn'd, and seen, and lov'd.

A CANTATA

RECITATIVE

The sun was in his highest strength
When Chloe grac'd the earth ;
The day was at its utmost length,
No night at Chloe's birth.

ARIA

The meads were mown, white roses blown,
All nature did conspire
To welcome here the shining lass,
The beauty of whose charming face
Sets all mankind on fire.

Where'er she moves ten thousand loves
Fan our souls with fond desire ;
We view with pleasure and amaze,
But Ah ! so surely as we gaze,
So surely we expire.

One fault she had some time ago,
Alas ! she would not hear ;
But now she's all perfection grown,
Despairing swains may make their moan,
And hope she'll lend an ear.

Th'Arabian bird a Phoenix gives,
And Venus in her Cupid lives,
And both in Chloe's eyes.
Nothing so rare but yields its like,
Or else it never dies.

THE HAPPY SWAIN

A Cantata

RECITATIVE

As Damon watch'd his harmless sheep
  Within a silent shade,
Lock'd in the bands of downy sleep
  He saw his charmer laid,
And thus he hail'd the beauteous maid.

AIR

  Close not those charming eyes,
  My life, my only dear !
  'Tis night till they arise,
  'Tis day when they appear.

RECIT.

Charm'd with the tuneful accents of his voice,
The lovely virgin rear'd her head,
For Damon's song made sorrow's self rejoice,
So sweet, 'twould e'en recall the dead :
Nor was the nymph coquette or coy ;
Too well she knew the artless boy.
With fervour not to be express'd
She clasp'd him to her snowy breast,
Who thus sang forth his joy.

AIR

  While in her arms my charmer holds me
  I think the queen of love enfolds me ;
  Less lovely Venus is than she,
  Adonis far less blest than me.

THE CENSORIOUS LOVER

A Cantata

RECITATIVE

Bright Teraminta cross'd the grove
Attended by a virgin train,
To wed a shepherd of the plain,
Whose wealth had got the upper hand of love.
Her fav'rite swain whom most she priz'd
She pass'd regardless by,
Who, thus forsaken and despis'd,
Did to her seeming scorn reply,

AIR

For trusting a creature
Inconstant by nature
I'm rightly rewarded.
The more we are faithful,
The more they're ungrateful,
The less we're regarded.

RECIT.

Touch'd by remorse, she left her train,
And caught him in the railing strain ;
She turn'd his torments to a jest,
While thus the swain his joy express'd.

AIR

There is no measure
To my pleasure
When thou art in my arms ;
To fix thee there
I'd laugh at fear,
And triumph in alarms.

THE ARTFUL SHEPHERDESS

A Cantata

RECITATIVE

The fair Pastora
Sat in a shady grove,
With Coridon her darling swain
Prostrate before her.
A thousand tales of love the shepherd told,
But the relentless fair,
With air disdainful,
Thus answered all his protestations.

AIR

The groves, the plains,
The nymphs, the swains,
The silver streams, the cooling shade,
All, all declare
How false you are,
How many hearts you have betray'd.
Ungrateful, go ;
Too well I know
Your fatal, false, deluding art ;
To ev'ry she
As well as me
You make an off'ring of your heart.

SLOW AIR

Yes, I will leave you, cruel maid ;
Your dread command shall be obey'd ;
But know, thou charming tyrant, know,
From you to certain death I go.

This said, with eyes expressing deadly resolution,
The melancholy shepherd took his leave.
The artful shepherdess is at a stand ;
Resolv'd, howe'er she will not lose him so,
With looks alluring and a syren voice
   She kindly thus recalls him.

AIR

   Turn, turn again,
   My dearest swain.
Gentler usage you shall find.
   You have my heart,
   But want the art
Of truly reading womankind.

A CANTATA

Where shall a poor, forsaken virgin fly,
To live at ease, or else in peace to die ?
To yonder hill I fain would go,
Where sporting lambkins play ;
Their innocence may sooth my woe,
And drive my grief away.

O, that I might retire
To some delightful shade,
Where love's pernicious fire
Can ne'er my rest invade.
See, there my Strephon walks along ;
To Phyllis he directs his song ;
To her alone he does resign
Those vows, those oaths
Which once were mine.

ON THE DEATH OF THE LATE FAMOUS MR. ELFORD[1]

A Cantata

RECITATIVE

Ask not Apollo's tuneful train
Why thus they weep and thus complain ?
'Tis Strephon's loss inspires their woe,
And fills with grief the world below.
The warbling nightingale, deprest,
Lodges sorrow in its breast ;
The lark which Strephon made so gay
Has ceas'd to sing since he has been away.

AIR

All nature's joys we lose in thee,
O thou the soul of harmony.
Burst, burst ye strings from ev'ry lyre,
And let your charms with him expire.

RECIT.

Could we believe that Strephon would remain
When royal Anna had forsook the plain ?
Soon to the Heav'ns above he did pursue,
His wonted musick to renew.
There to his blessed patroness[2] does he
Chaunt forth eternal melody,
And, for a while, the heavenly choir
Stand mute, to be delighted and admire.

AIR

In those peaceful realms above
All is musick, all is love.
Ever tuneful, ever gay,
Eternal bliss, eternal day.

*The six following Cantatas after the Italian manner
are imitated and contracted from as many stories of Ovid*

CANTATA I

VENUS AND ADONIS

Soon as the infant sun had deck'd the skies,
With eager haste Adonis did arise ;
O'er meadows tipp'd with morning dew
The sprightly shepherd nimbly flew,
And thus the wanton boy
In sweetest tones express'd his joy.

AIR

Chrystal streams like silver shining,
Blended branches softly twining,
Smiling plains and verdant groves,
Are objects that Adonis loves.

Let silly shepherds court despair
And languish for some cruel fair ;
Uncommon bliss I here enjoy,
Too calm to kill, too sweet to cloy.

RECITATIVE

A savage boar came o'er the plain,
And rudely tore the hapless swain,
Who, struggling, call'd for help in vain.
His cries were heard by beauty's chief,
Who nimbly flew to his relief ;
But when she found him dead, she thus express'd
    her grief.

AIR

Let dire destruction quickly fall
On Heav'n, on earth, on me and all ;
Let lightning flash, let thunder roar,
Since dear Adonis is no more.

Unhinge, unhinge, ye starry spheres ;
Let grating discord fill my ears ;
Let flames devouring all destroy,
Since I have lost my darling boy.

CANTATA II

APOLLO AND DAPHNE

RECIT.

Wild as despair the tim'rous Daphne flew,
While amorous Phoebus closely did pursue ;
But when the god had follow'd long in vain,
At last in soft melodious strain
He thus essay'd the cruel fair to gain :

AIR

Dearest Daphne, do not fly me,
All thy needless fears remove ;
Do not, do not thus deny me,
But reward Apollo's love.
When unconstant men are wooers
Virgins may maintain the field,
But when gods become pursuers
Ev'ry fair should gladly yield.

RECIT.

This said, he rudely seiz'd the trembling maid,
Who loudly call'd to Heav'n for aid ;
When, Lo ! by pow'r divine she grew
A laurel, ever blooming, ever new,
From whose immortal trunk these accents came,
His frustrate hopes to mock, his love to blame.

AIR

Phoebus, while you're such a rover
Small success in love you'll find ;
Till you are grown a constant lover
Virgins never will be kind.
Leave this wanton way of wooing,
Fickle courtship is but vain ;
While you all are thus pursuing
You perhaps may none obtain.

CANTATA III

JUPITER AND LEDA

RECIT.

In silver plumes of snowy down array'd,
Great Jove to Leda came,
And while she fondly with his pinions play'd
Thus sang the beauteous dame.

AIR

Purling streams and crystal fountains,
All to thee their beauties owe,
Nor can whitest Alpine mountains
Rival thee in whiter snow.

Thou to me art always dear,
I adore thy downy charms ;
Ever take thy dwelling here ;
Never fly from Leda's arms.

RECIT.

As thus she sang almighty Jove
Explor'd the sweets of godlike love,
And while he warmly touch'd her heart
She thus express'd the pleasing smart.

AIR

Dearest charmer, O forbear !
I can ne'er such joys receive ;
This is bliss beyond compare,
Nor could gods a greater give.

Tho' the streams thy absence mourn,
Let 'em, let 'em mourn in vain ;
Thou shalt never hence return,
But with Leda still remain.

CANTATA IV

PARIS AND OENONE

RECIT.

When Paris bore away the Grecian prize,
Waiting on Ida's top with longing eyes
OEnone stood,
And when she view'd
The Trojan fleet approaching sail along,
She strove to charm her shepherd to the shore
With this melodious song.

167

AIR

Welcome, welcome, dearest swain,
Welcome to these groves again,
And to OEnone's arms.

Leave the raging, stormy sea,
Come and spend thy days with me
In endless peaceful charms.

RECIT.

The zephyrs caught the charming sound,
And echo made her strains rebound,
But cruel Paris sail'd along
Regardless of the tuneful song,
While thus she sang to ease her pain
And call the shepherd back again.

AIR

Tell me, Paris, tell me, why
You from my embraces fly
With such impetuous haste.

Cruel shepherd, you've undone me ;
Tell me, Paris, why you shun me,
And faithless prove at last.

CANTATA V

VERTUMNUS AND POMONA

RECIT.

Transform'd in female shape, as old and lame,
The god Vertumnus to Pomona came,
And while the goddess all her store display'd,
He thus address'd the heavenly maid.

AIR

Goddess lovely and divine,
Guardian of each fruitful tree,
A while thy darling joys decline,
And lend an ear to love and me.

Blooming beauties should be kind
And take the blessings while they may,
For time is swift, and love is blind,
And passion cools when charms decay.

RECIT.

While he appear'd thus odious to her eyes,
The goddess did his strains despise ;
But when transform'd by pow'r divine,
Vertumnus did with blooming graces shine,
Thus sang Pomona all amaz'd,
While on the youthful god she fondly gaz'd.

AIR

Successful, happy charmer,
'Tis you alone can warm her,
Who never lov'd before.

Be bless'd as I can make you,
I never will forsake you,
But love you more and more.

CANTATA VI

CYNTHIA AND ENDYMION

RECIT.

The silver moon serenely shone,
And night appear'd as day ;
But e'er her course was well begun
She rudely stole away.

AIR

Gentle orb of radiant fire,
Sweet adorner of the night,
Why dost thou in glooms retire
And conceal thy sacred light?

Scorching Phoebus all the day
Reigns with too tyrannic heat;
But fair Cynthia's milder sway
Is the shepherd's sole retreat.

RECIT.

Thus in a melancholy glade
Endymion hail'd the heavenly maid,
Whose beams forsook the clouds with joyful pride
While to the swain the goddess thus reply'd.

AIR

Shepherd, cease this fond complaining;
Do not thus ungrateful prove;
You 'gainst Cynthia are exclaiming,
While for you she burns for love.

Bless this happy, kind occasion,
Bless your more prevailing charms,
That, without the least persuasion,
Yield a goddess to your arms.

CALLIOPE TO HER SKYLARK

Inscrib'd to Alexander Pope, Esq.

Hush, my little tuneful dear !
Cease to flutter, cease to fear ;
Here serenely take thy rest ;
In my bosom build thy nest.

Full secure and far remote
From the raven's croaking note,
Or the hideous hoot of owls,
Or the din of midnight fowls.

These have seen with envious eyes
Thee, my charmer, soar the skies ;
And, with most reluctant ears,
Heard thee warble through the spheres.

Higher flights and loftier lays
Must, of course, their envy raise,
For the sweeter thou dost sing,
Rancour feels the deeper sting.

Thus the damn'd in shades below,
Conscious of eternal woe,
At the joys of Heaven's blest train,
Gnash their teeth, but all in vain.

WRITTEN IN A GARDEN BY MOONLIGHT

See, smiling Cynthia now begins to rise,
And with transparent glories paints the skies.
Hail beauteous rival of the darksome night,
Whose glooms give way to thy superior light.
Thy lucid charms afford a second day,
And guide the weary pilgrim on his way.
Thy milder presence renders open plains
Delightful to the nymphs and to the swains,
Who all the day in lonely shades retreat,
To shun the fury of meridian heat.

The warbling lark forsakes its downy nest,
And thinks the day in Cynthia's smiles express'd ;
Beguil'd by thee he chaunts his morning song,
The tuneful summons to the wakeful throng.
All nature takes th'alarm ; the fish forsake
The deep recesses of the silent lake,
And on the surface of the floods are seen,
While wanton lambkins sport upon the green.
The fairy elves assemble in a ring ;
By Cynthia's silver light they dance and sing ;
Beneath her gentle influence sport and play,
And nothing fear but the returning day.

AN ODE IN PRAISE OF CHASTITY

Let slaves and brutes by raging lust possess'd
Harbour in each polluted breast
A dire, infectuous flame, which burns
Fierce and insensible, a flame which turns
Our godlike soul, divine and bright,
The source of virtue and of light,
Into a canker'd gloom, and baleful night.

Let the infatuate, wretched soul
In fulsome blisses fondly roll,
Despise advice, and dare controul.

Let all go on as nature leads ;
O'er verdant plains, and flow'ry meads
My dear lov'd nymph and I will walk,
While in diverting, harmless talk
We in each other's soul a bliss enjoy
That ne'er will fade, and never, never cloy.

AN ODE IN PRAISE OF COFFEE

Thou sacred liquour of nectarous taste,
O Coffee ! thou whose fame shall last
While o'er thy glowing charms we smile,
And bless the product of thy parent soil ;
When spleen and all its direful train
Despotick vex my tortur'd brain,
Thy presence makes the bold usurpers fly,
Leaving my peaceful soul possess'd of calm serenity.

Charm'd with thy scent, and by thy help reviv'd,
When of my reason I'm deprived
By the prevailing charms of wine,
Or glorious Punch, as equally divine,
Thy healing virtues soon destroy
Whatever can my sense annoy.
But who, Ah ! who can tell how those are blest
Who share the pleasures thou bestow'st to crown a
plenteous feast.

THE REFINERS OF MANKIND

Charming tea, enchanting liquour,
Makes dear scandal flow the quicker ;
Polishes the rough by nature,
To the prude it lends keen satire,
Helps politest conversation,
And gives glory to a nation.

Sword and sceptre, mace and mitre,
Can they pass their time politer
Than in parties at quadrille,
Basto, Punto, and Spadille ?
These refine and make men civil ;
Vulgar Cribbage is the devil.

174

THE HUNTSMAN'S ROUSE

The hounds are all out, and the morning does peep,
Why, how now, you sluggardly sot !
How can you lie snoring asleep while we all
A-horseback have got, my dear boy, my brave boy,
While we all a-horseback have got.

I cannot get up, for the overnight cup
So terribly lies in my head ;
Beside, my wife cries, My dear, do not rise,
But cuddle me longer in bed, my dear boy,
But cuddle me longer in bed.

Come, on with your boots, and saddle your mare,
Nor tire us with longer delay ;
The cry of the hounds and the sight of the hare
Will chase all our vapours away, my dear boys,
Will chase all our vapours away.

THE STAGG AT BAY

A Hunting Song in " Apollo and Daphne "[1]

Sung by Mr. Ray, in the Character of a Huntsman

Away, away, the stagg's at bay,
The hounds are waiting for their prey ;
The huntsman's call invites ye all ;
Come in, come in, boys, while you may.

The horn shall be the marry'd man's fee,
And let him take it not in scorn ;
The great and sage in ev'ry age
Have not disdain'd to wear the horn.

The jolly horn, the rosy morn,
The harmony of deep-mouth'd hounds :
These, these, my boys, are heavenly joys ;
A sportsman's pleasure knows no bounds.

A PASTORAL

Leave, leave your folded flocks in peace to sleep ;
All night upon the green your revels keep ;
While on the verdant plain we sport and play
We'll never think of sleep or wish for day.
With innocent pleasure our moments we'll measure,
Content is a treasure that ne'er will decay.
Tho' wordlings advise us, tho' lordlings despise us,
They wrongly surmise us ; we're better than they.

THE HAPPY RUSTICS

In these shades with delightful tranquillity,
   Free from envy, care, and strife,
Blest with innocence, health, and agility,
   O, how sweet's a rural life !

Endless circles of pleasure surrounding us,
   Ever easy, ever gay,
No perplexities ever confounding us,
   Thus our moments slide away.

No ambition without its anxiety ;
   Crowns themselves are lin'd with care ;
Sweet content is sufficient variety ;
   More is but the miser's share.

THE STORY OF UNFORTUNATE PHYLLIS

Colin a gentle shepherd swain,
  With ev'ry virtue grac'd,
Upon the fairest of the plain
  His fond affection plac'd.

Young Phyllis, beautiful and gay,
  By all ador'd and lov'd,
Had stol'n the shepherd's heart away,
  But mark how Phyllis prov'd.

Deaf and regardless to his prayer,
  With scorn she from him flew ;
She was unkind as she was fair,
  And false as he was true.

Poor Colin, forc'd by her disdain,
  To desarts wild retir'd,
Where oft he sigh'd, but sigh'd in vain
  For her whom he admir'd.

Tho' other nymphs for Colin pin'd
  Phyllis his love despis'd ;
And to that passion was unkind
  Which many would have priz'd.

But she, who had thus long deny'd
  An humble, constant swain,
Phyllis, who had with wond'rous pride
  Resisted all the plain.

Was vanquish'd by a coat of lace,
  And by an outside won ;
By flaxen wig and brazen face
  Poor Phyllis was undone.

It chanc'd a splendid courtier came
  To breathe the rural air,
Whose gay addresses did inflame
  This too, too easy fair.

This courtier, artful to deceive,
  So much on Phyllis gain'd,
All he could ask or she could give
  He easily obtain'd.

But scarce had he the fair enjoy'd,
  And gain'd her tender heart,
When, with her fond embraces cloy'd,
  He slyly did depart.

Phyllis thus basely left alone
  By him whom she ador'd,
To ev'ry echo made her moan,
  And ev'ry pow'r implor'd.

But Ah ! Alas ! too late she found
  Her darling so unkind,
For love had all their labours crown'd,
  And left a pledge behind.

Of Colin now she seeks relief,
  And to the desart flies
Where he had stol'n to vent his grief
  And echo forth his cries.

But Colin, grown much wiser now,
    Experienc'd by his smart,
Met Phyllis with an angry brow,
    And baffl'd all her art.

His love was now to hatred turn'd,
    His fondness to disdain ;
And she who had his passion scorn'd
    He scorn'd as much again.

Back to the groves he did repair,
    And there in wedlock join'd
A nymph as faithless Phyllis fair,
    But much more chaste and kind.

Poor Phyllis far remoter fled,
    Her adverse fate to blame,
Where she conceal'd her guilty head,
    But not her grief and shame.

A PASTORAL MADE IN THE YEAR 1715

    Flocks are sporting,
    Doves are courting,
Warbling linnets sweetly sing ;
    Joy and pleasure
    Without measure,
Kindly hail the glorious spring.

    Flocks are bleating,
    Rocks repeating,
Valleys echo back the sound ;
    Dancing, singing,
    Piping, springing,
Nought but mirth and joy goes round.

THE AGREABLE SURPRISE

On a sultry summer's day
Hyacintha sleeping lay,
Hid within a verdant shade,
For serenest slumbers made.

Coridon, her darling swain,
As he walk'd along the plain,
Saw the dear, the beauteous maid
In a tempting posture laid.

To her side he softly crept,
And prest and kiss'd her as she slept,
Then gently whisper'd in her ear,
But she did not, or would not hear.

At length he boldly jogged his fair,
Who, waking, blush'd to find him there;
She strove to rise, and had been gone,
But that the shepherd kept her down.

MUSICK'S VICTORY,

OR

THE BAFFL'D POET

While fair Pastora sat with me
Beneath a shady myrtle tree,
My warbling muse in sweetest lays
Sung my passion and her praise,

Till the divine seraphick lyre
Set her glowing breast on fire ;
Raptur'd she heard th'enchanting strains,
And vow'd she lov'd me 'bove all swains.

But young Endymion brought his lute
Which struck my muse, my numbers mute ;
No more she lik'd my late lov'd song,
But wish'd she might sit all day long
To hear the blest Endymion.

Thus musick drew her soul away ;
Enchanting musick won the day.

THE VIRGIN'S ADDRESS

To Pallas the celestial maid
A virtuous nymph devoutly pray'd
For all those gifts that could refine
And make a virgin more divine ;
The smiling goddess thus replied,
Mortal, your suit is not deny'd ;
I give you an industrious hand
The skillful needle to command.

The tender grass, the blooming trees,
The crystal streams, the briny seas,
Fragrant flowers, groves and plains,
And all the spacious world contains
Shall in soft shades be wrought by you,
And kept for everlasting view.

This art alone will crown your pains
With constant praises, certain gains,
While you, secure from sloth and pride,
Herein have all that you can wish beside.

THE BLESSINGS OF PEACE

Let ev'ry face be fill'd with joy
   And ev'ry glass with wine ;
Let boundless mirth all cares destroy
   In ecstasies divine.

For peace and plenty are returning
   To our British Isle ;
Then lay aside all grief and mourning,
   Gayly ever smile.

Our gracious Queen, our loyal Peers
   And Commons have agreed
That wars shall cease for future years,
   And union shall succeed.

Rejoice, ye beauties of the court,
   Your heroes will return ;
Ye British nymphs, no more resort
   In lonely shades to mourn.

For now your faithful swains shall bless
   Your long neglected arms
With glory, honour, and success,
   And never dying charms.

While you, with peaceful blessings crown'd,
   Enjoy the sweets of love,
And new-born pleasures still abound
   In ev'ry blissful grove.

Ye martial heroes, lay aside
   The thoughts of war's alarms ;
Your hours will better be employ'd
   Within the fair one's arms.

They shall with equal transports meet
   While boldly you advance,
And make your pleasures doubly sweet
   With endless complaisance.

While you recruit an infant train
   In Venus' gentler wars
To make amends for those you've slain
   Within the field of Mars.

Ye loyal Britons, lay aside
   All grief and discontent ;
Your Queen will such a peace provide
   Shall all your fears prevent.

Great Anna seeks our happiness,
   And not her private ends ;
To find out means her realm to bless
   Is all that she intends.

Let, then, the happy world rejoice,
   Let war and discord cease ;
Let ev'ry heart and ev'ry voice
   Applaud this glorious peace.

A RHAPSODY ON PEACE

Eternal Father, Son, and Holy Ghost,
Appear, encompass'd by a glorious host
Of saints and angels ; let the tuneful spheres
With harmony celestial charm our ears ;
Let all the various parts of nature's voice,
In one exulting tone, aloud rejoice.
And while our aching eyes are fix'd on High,
Upon the glory of thy majesty,
Great God of peace, look down, and smiling show
How pleas'd thou art, when union is below.

A HYMN

Inspir'd with ecstasies divine,
How gladly would I strive to raise
This faint, aspiring voice of mine
To sing my great creator's praise.

Hither, ye hosts of winged angels fly,
Descend in glitt'ring legions from the sky.
Come, join with me and teach me how to sing
Some grateful hymn to my almighty King.

Smiling cherubs, haste away
From your realms of endless day ;
Join your warbling notes with mine,
To make the off'ring more divine.

Thus on the wings of harmony and love
My raptur'd soul with swiftest haste shall move,
Till, borne above the earth by fierce desire,
I add to the divine celestial choir.

ANOTHER HYMN

This world's a vale of sin, and all below
Is sorrow, vanity and woe ;
All things which here on earth I see
Are full of folly, sin, and misery.

Dearest Saviour, O convey me
    To Thy Father's arms.
Let not this vain world betray me
    With its fond alarms.

I mount, I fly, I scale the sky,
The world and Satan I defy ;
With God and Christ I shall remain,
Never to return again.

ON THE DEATH OF A PRETTY INFANT

How justly may we mourn our mortal state,
And blame the rigid hand of partial fate,
Since even tender infants are not free
From the unerring stroke of destiny !
But smiling babes as well are snatch'd away
As aged souls, who live but to decay.
Else had Eliza liv'd till wit and grace
Had made her mind as charming as her face ;
Till rip'ning beauty would have made her shine
All innocent, all lovely and divine.
But now no more Eliza's name we hear
Without the mournful tribute of a tear.
All mourn Eliza's loss, her parents most,
Since they in her have all their comfort lost.
But see, her dear, her infant soul arise
In eager triumph through the distant skies ;
See what a shining cloud the Heav'ns display
To meet Eliza in the Milky Way.
Why, then, should we lament that she's above ?
'Tis true, it shows our reverence and love ;
But yet we ought a sympathy to bear,
And while she's blest in Heav'n, we should be joyful
  here.

THE DISTRESS'D FATHER,

OR

THE AUTHOR'S TEARS OVER HIS DEAR DAUGHTER RACHEL[1]

Oh ! lead me where my darling lies,
  Cold as the marble stone ;
I will recall her with my cries,
  And wake her with my moan.

Come from thy bed of clay, my dear,
  See where thy father stands ;
His soul he sheds out tear by tear,
  And wrings his wretched hands.

But Ah ! Alas ! thou can'st not rise,
  Alas ! thou can'st not hear,
Or at thy tender father's cries
  Thou surely would'st appear.

Since, then, my love, my soul's delight,
  Thou can'st not come to me,
Rather than want thy pleasing sight
  I'll dig my way to thee.

THE AFORESAID CHILD, DYING ON HER FATHER'S BIRTHDAY, OCCASION'D THE FOLLOWING LINES

That fatal day, which lent my earliest breath,
Gave my dear girl to the cold arms of death :
Others in triumph may their birthdays keep ;
Mine calls aloud for tears, and bids me weep.

ON THE DEATH OF MRS. ANNE CLEEVE

One of the Best of Women

Ye reverend Manes of the ancient dead,
Whose pious urns have unmolested lain
A long eternity of buried years,
Num'rous as are the tributary tears
Which grace your memories ; arise and stand
In sacred column on the heavenly strand,
To welcome to your realms of endless rest
As bright a soul as e'er was render'd blest.

For surely such is she who now is gone
To reap the blessings of the heavenly throne.
She was . . . but Ah ! Alas ! she is no more . . .
That virtue's self which we should all adore.

A tender parent and a faithful wife
In ev'ry action of her pious life ;
A worthy mistress and a real friend ;
But . . . what we never can enough commend . . .
Is that this most divine, this matchless She
Was ev'n the very soul of charity ;
To all good works most zealously sincere,
To all ill thoughts and actions so severe ;
In short, she was most justly these, and all
We may consummately religious call.

But Ah ! her virtues will adorn her hearse
More than the vain efforts of feeble verse,
Which but augments the grief of each sad mind
That she has left to mourn her here behind.
Cease, then, impatient muse, and leave the rest
To be in silence and in tears express'd.

ON THE DEATH OF
MRS. ELIZABETH FARRINGTON

If to observe religion's strictest laws
Merits reward in Heav'n, or earth's applause,
Eliza must be bless'd, her shade rever'd,
In whom the finish'd saint so bright appear'd ;
In ev'ry action of her pious life
A virtuous, prudent, and a tender wife ;
A mother most indulgent, and a friend
Constant, sincere, and gen'rous to the end.
The careful mistress of a well rul'd house,
The dear lov'd wife of an endearing spouse ;
Fond mother of a numerous, beauteous line,
Whom all lament, but none can e'er outshine.

EPITAPH INTENDED FOR
MRS. SUSANNAH WORSDALE[1]

Who Died Young

So fair a face, so exquisite a mind,
Such innocence with so much beauty join'd,
Heav'n thought too good for earth, so call'd her hence,
To places fit for so much excellence.

ON THE NEVER ENOUGH TO BE LAMENTED
DEATH OF MY DEAR FRIEND,
MR. ROBERT CHESBY

Who play'd to the last Perfection on the Violin

O, hadst thou liv'd to let the world have seen
How great, how glorious thou in time hadst been,
We had not griev'd so much ; but Ah ! we find
Thou wast by Heaven for nobler ends design'd ;
The sacred consort of the heavenly sphere
Was but imperfect while my friend was here ;
'Twas for that reason thou wast call'd above,
To grace those realms of endless bliss and love
With never ceasing harmony ; to show
Their musick now exceedeth ours below.

THE CYPRESS GROVE,
OR
THE POET'S TEARS OVER HIS DEPARTED FRIENDS, AND
FIRST TO THE MEMORY OF HIS EVER HONOUR'D MASTER,
MR. OLAUS WESTEINSON LINNERT,[1] COMMONLY CALL'D
WESTEN, WHO GAVE HIM HIS FIRST NOTIONS OF
COMPOSITION

If weeping could to life his shade restore
I'd drain my eyestrings to recall my master,
The best of men, of friends and of musicians ;
For so I found him, who, with gen'rous pity,
When like an infant wandering and forlorn
My infant muse of all implor'd assistance,
He only show'd compassion to her cries,
Fost'ring the wretch with a paternal fondness.
He made her his adopted darling charge,
Rang'd into order her confus'd ideas,
Corrected her mistakes by friendly reason,
And taught her ev'n to think.   Shall, then, the muse
Leave him unsung by whose fond care she sings ?

Or, vainly to herself her rise ascribing,
Suffer his name to vanish in oblivion ?
No, as the labour and the toil were his,
Be his the glory ; let the grateful muse
Attempt a name but for her Westein's sake,
That when it shall be said, in times succeeding,
(For, like the Phoenix, does the poet's fame
Rise from his ashes) that she well has sung,
He too may be a partner in the praise.

THE APOTHEOSIS

Of the Most Noble Edmund Sheffield, Duke of
Buckingham, who died at Rome the 30th day of
October, 1735, and now lies entombed in Westminster
Abbey.

    Immortal pow'rs who rule above,
        A soul sublime receive
    To realms of endless peace and love,
        While we survive to grieve.

    His sacred shade, ye angels, guide
        To everlasting rest,
    While kindred gods with joy and pride
        All hail their welcome guest.

    Oh ! he was nature's wonder,
        All goodness, mildness, truth ;
    Torn are our hearts asunder
        To lose so sweet a youth.

    Heav'n has his worth rewarded
        With all its blissful store ;
    Earth has his fame recorded
        Till time shall be no more.

THE MUSE'S TEARS

Esteem'd when living, and when dead recorded ;
So should a faithful servant be rewarded.

An elegiac Ode to the Memory of that sober,
ingenious youth, Mr. Richard Osborne,[1] educated by
the Author, and lamented by all. He died Dec. 22,
1736, in the nineteenth year of his age.

> Where is my soul's chief comfort flown,
>   Where vanish'd all my joy ?
> Sure grief like mine was never known ;
>   I've lost my darling boy.
>
> Oh ! he was art and nature's pride :
>   So sweet a form and mind
> Were ne'er before so near allied,
>   Or in one person join'd.
>
> Pure were his thoughts, his words sincere,
>   His actions just and true :
> To him was virtue ever dear,
>   For vice he never knew.
>
> Musick was all his soul's delight,
>   And learning all his store ;
> His constant study day and night
>   Was still to gain the more.
>
> Gifts so sublime in one so young
>   To future time shall shine ;
> And tell, when these sad strains are sung,
>   How great a loss was mine.

TO THE RIGHT HONOURABLE RICHARD, EARL OF BURLINGTON[1]

O Burlington, to ev'ry muse endear'd,
Behold the bard by thy bright influence chear'd ;
Easy his life and unconstrain'd his lays,
While his warm heart glows grateful to thy praise.
He finds his genius with his fortunes mend,
And knows the cause, for Burlington's his friend.

TO THE RIGHT HONOURABLE CHARLES, VISCOUNT BRUCE[1]

Where shall the sister arts protection find
But from the best and noblest of mankind ?
Without such patrons science would decay,
And in oblivion moulder quite away :
The age would be of reason's light bereft,
Were not, like you, some bright examples left,
Who nourish learning, patronize our schools,
And rescue truth from the assaults of fools.
By your most godlike acts the world is told
That Bruce is what Maecenas was of old :
Like him from heroes sprung and ancient kings,
You feed afresh the Heliconian springs,
Relieve affliction, bid the poet live,
Bless'd in that bounty you delight to give.
Amazing goodness ! greatly to bestow,
And not the person, but the motive know :
To such high worth the muse presumes to raise
This monument of gratitude and praise.

SIR WILLIAM'S BIRTHDAY

Joy awakes with the festival morn
When the worthiest of mortals was born.
Let him reign the chief toast of the night,
While we mention his name with delight.
So here's to his health,
Peace, pleasure and wealth
Surrounding, abounding, attend all his days.
Let flatt'rers of state
Toast only the great,
True merit like his has most claim to our praise.

Let his consort next crown the full glass ;
Ever cheerfully round let it pass.
By our glad acclamations let's show
What to beauty and virtue we owe.
So here's to her health,
Peace, pleasure and wealth
Surrounding, abounding, attend all her days.
Let flatt'rers of state
Toast only the great,
True merit like hers has most claim to our praise.

Let their progeny next be our toast,
Long to live their delight and their boast,
And immortalize Abdy, a name
Ever dear in the records of fame.
So here's to their health,
Peace, pleasure and wealth
Surrounding, abounding, attend all their days.
Let flatt'rers of state
Toast only the great,
True merit like theirs has most claim to our praise.

THE LAUREL GROVE,

OR

THE POET'S TRIBUTE TO MUSICK AND MERIT, AND FIRST TO MR. GEORGE FREDERICK HANDEL

Hail ! unexhausted source of harmony,
Thou glorious chief of Phoebus tuneful sons,
In whom the knowledge of all magick numbers
Or sound melodious does concentred dwell.
The envy and the wonder of mankind
Must terminate, but never can thy lays ;
For when, absorb'd in elemental flame,
This world shall vanish, musick shall exist.
Then thy sweet strains, to native skies returning,
Shall breathe in songs of seraphims and angels,
Commixt and lost in harmony eternal,
That fills all Heaven. . . .

TO MY STUDIOUS FRIEND, MR. JOHN FREDERICK LAMPE[1]

Call not my Lampe obscure because unknown.
He shines in secret now, to friends alone ;
Light him but up, let him in publick blaze,
He will delight not only, but amaze.

TO MR. JOHN STANLEY

*The Wonderful Blind Youth, Organist of St. Andrew's,
Holborn*

Why do mistaken mortals call thee blind ?
Thine eyes are but inverted to thy mind ;
There thou explorest ideas unconfin'd,
Whilst we, who look before, are dark behind.

TO MR. OBADIAH SHUTTLEWORTH[1]

*Made and Spoken Extempore, on Hearing him Perform
a Solo of Corelli with great Propriety*

Envy of foreigners, thy country's pride,
Whose soul is harmony, nor ought beside,
Oh ! could Corelli hear thy charming lays,
He'd hug thee in his arms, and give thee praise ;
For thou such justice to his works hast done,
He need not blush to own thee for a son.

TO THE MEMORY OF MR. GEORGE HAYDEN[1]

Author of many Excellent Compositions in Musick

Hayden, these little legacies of thine
Glow with the tincture of a worth divine ;
The master shines in all that thou hast done,
And Envy's self must now thy merit own.
I lov'd thee living, and thy shade revere ;
What more but silence and a friendly tear ?

TO MR. MATTHEW DUBOURG[1]

At Dublin

So fine a genius and so great a hand,
Nature and art, Dubourg, are at a stand ;
On thee they have bestow'd their richest store ;
Can we expect, or can'st thou wish for more ?

TO MR. GALLIARD[1]

On his Setting a Hymn of Milton

Galliard, each note that flows from thee
Is like thyself, polite and free.
Thy genius, generous and gay,
Warms like July, and blooms like May.
Thou hast new-plum'd our Milton's wings,
Who now not only soars, but sings.

TO MR. GEMINIANI[1]

At the Hague

Geminiani ! 'tis not land or sea
Can bar the grateful muse from following thee ;
Fly where thou wilt, she shall as quick pursue,
And sing the praises to thy merit due.
In my mind's eye I still enjoy thee here,
Still hold thee in my heart and in my ear.
Proud to adorn this verse with thy great name,
Thus thy disciple builds on thee his fame.

TO DR. PEPUSCH[1]

Lovers and connoisseurs of sound agree
That musick's art, Pepusch, owes much to thee,
For thou, a painful champion in her cause,
Hast methodis'd her controverted laws.
Thy long unwearied labour and deep thought
Her problems have to demonstration brought,
Whose rules, unerring, such conviction give,
That till the science dies thy name must live.

TO MR. THOMAS ROSEINGRAVE[1]

Organist of St. George's, Hanover Square,
To whose friendly instruction I am much indebted

Rouse, Roseingrave, assert thy deathless name,
And stand thou in the foremost rank of fame,
Since all the sons of harmony confess
Thy solid fugues thy solid thoughts express.
Let finger-mongers deal discordant noise
To fat churchwardens and to 'prentice boys ;
Be they the Sunday idols of the crowd,
Who value nought but what is light and loud.
Give me my Roseingrave, my soul to raise,
Who, with his solemn and judicial lays
Adds sacred fervour to our pray'r and praise.

THE ENGLISH PROTESTANT

Inscrib'd to John Lloyd, Esq.

I am an Englishman, and dare be free ;
Tory and Whig are both alike to me :
Such shifts, such dirty work I see in either,
I fully am determin'd to be neither.
That slavish trick I leave to knaves and fools,
The statesmen's easy gulls, or servile tools.
Papist or Protestant, or bond or free,
Those, Lloyd, are all distinctions known to me :
The pattern thou of what mankind should be.

THE TRUE WOMAN'S MAN

Inscrib'd to George Rivers, Esq.

In the opinion of the vulgar crowd
No merit is to women's men allow'd,
But tattling, dandling, loit'ring all the day,
And trifling life's most precious hours away.
Let such as these, when caught in wedlock's snare,
Be the coquette or stern virago's share ;
But to a girl of honour, worth and sense
Let no such coxcomb dare to make pretence.
Be hers the gay, the generous, the brave,
No surly tyrant, nor yet henpeck'd slave ;
But one who will instruct, approve, defend,
A constant lover and a faithful friend,
Who, by his conduct, shall acquire such fame,
She shall with pride and pleasure wear his name.
The ladies now, methinks, the bard surround,
And cry, *Where is this jewel to be found?*
I answer, she to whose blest lot thou'lt fall,
In thee, my Rivers, will possess 'em all.

THE HAPPY MARRIAGE

Inscrib'd to Nathaniel Oldham, Esq.[1]

Thrice blissful wedlock, where a beauteous wife
Kindly contributes to a social life ;
Where home is made delightful, where each friend
His option and her conduct must commend.
Such, Oldham, is thy choice, thy partner such.
She can't be prais'd, or thou approv'd too much.

LOVE MAKES THE POET

In Several Verses to the most Charming Lesbia

UPON FIRST SIGHT OF LESBIA

So many charms were never, sure,
   For one alone design'd.
The gods, to make you more complete,
   Have robb'd all womankind.

THE ADDRESS

To the Same

Thou fairest, most divine of womankind,
Angel in form, and goddess in thy mind,
I've seen you, charmer ; that alone will prove
As I have seen, so I, of course, must love.
I own I merit no-one so divine,
But yet, if love is merit, you are mine.
Then to my fate the last decision give ;
Or frown me into dust, or smile, and bid me live.

LESBIA'S APPROACH

Stop, Phoebus, stop thy swift career,
And know the charming Lesbia's here ;
When she is absent we admire
The glories of thy sacred fire,
But when she comes, for shame, retire.

BEAUTY PEERLESS

While in my Lesbia's face I view
    A thousand thousand charms,
Still something lovely, something new
    My wondering soul alarms.

Strange pow'r, that nature should create
    One so divinely fair
That she no beauty can compleat
    With Lesbia to compare.

BEAUTY IN TEARS,

OR

LESBIA'S SQUIRREL

Come ev'ry fav'rite animal of all
We may a goddess or a beauty call,
Hither with expedious haste repair.
And with your loud complainings fill the ambient air.

Hither come and mourn with me
Pretty Puggy's destiny,
Puggy, the beauty of its kind approv'd,
Envy'd by swains, and by the nymphs belov'd.

Ye sporting Cupids who attend
Divine Cytherea's self, descend!
Descend, and see a weeping goddess bath
Her darling squirrel's corpse
In tears would buy an Alexander's death.

Come, come, around the beauteous Lesbia play,
And try a thousand wanton arts to drive her grief away.

ON LESBIA'S RECOVERY FROM A FIT OF SICKNESS

As when the god of light awhile retires,
And nightly shades conceal his sacred fires,
The drooping world laments that he's away,
And nature mourns the absence of the day;
But when re-usher'd by approaching morn,
And dazzling beams his glorious face adorn,
The universe in shining pomp appears,
And ev'ry face a mark of gladness wears;
So, when my Lesbia was with pain opprest,
And raging fevers rack'd her gentle breast,
With pity fill'd for the dear maid I love,
Her torments double to my soul did prove.
My Lesbia felt no pain, endur'd no smart
But what with mightier force opprest my bleeding
    heart.
But when relenting Fate had heard my pray'r,
And look'd with pity on the tortur'd fair;
When it had eas'd her of her racking pain,
And brought her to her pristine health again,
Witness, ye gods, what joys inspir'd my breast,
With what excess of transport was I blest.

My grief, which nothing could before compare,
Was equall'd by the joy my soul did share
In the recovery of my charming fair
Then Oh, ye pow'rs, would ye propitious prove
To chaste desires, and to constant love,
Bless her with lasting health whom I adore,
And make her mine, that I may ask no more.

LESBIA'S INSENSIBILITY

Observe the numerous stars which grace
    The fair expanded skies ;
So many charms has Lesbia's face,
    A thousand more her eyes.

Whene'er the beauteous maid appears
    We cannot but admire ;
But when she speaks she charms our ears
    And sets our souls on fire.

What pity 'tis a creature
    By nature form'd so fair,
Divine in ev'ry feature,
    Should give mankind despair.

She gazes all around her,
    And gains a thousand hearts,
But Cupid cannot wound her,
    For she has all his darts.

LESBIA'S CRUELTY

She whom above myself I do prize
Does me above all men despise ;
My faithful passion is so great,
Nothing exceeds it, but her hate.

Ye gods, must I for ever love ?
Must she for ever cruel prove ?
Must my torment, grief and pain
Meet with nothing but disdain ?

Turn, Ah, turn those eyes on me !
Look with pity on your swain ;
Either give me liberty,
Or forbear to give me pain.

ON LESBIA'S CRUELTY

In vain the god's endeavour
To mitigate my anguish,
Alas ! I still must languish
If Lesbia is unkind.

Now cruel maid, if ever,
Your tyranny give over,
Or soon your tortur'd lover
In death's cold arms you'll find.

ROGER AND DOLLY

Young Roger came tapping at Dolly's window,
    Tumpaty, tumpaty, tump.
He begg'd for admittance, she answer'd him, No !
    Glumpaty, glumpaty, glump.
My Dolly, my dear, your true love is here,
    Dumpaty, dumpaty, dump.
No, Roger, no, as you came you may go,
    Clumpaty, clumpaty, clump.

Oh ! what is the reason, dear Dolly, he cried,
    Pumpaty, pumpaty, pump.
That thus I'm cast off and unkindly deny'd,
    Frumpaty, frumpaty, frump.
Some rival more dear I guess has been here,
    Crumpaty, crumpaty, crump.
Suppose there's been two ; pray, sir, what's that to you ?
    Numpaty, numpaty, nump.

O, then with a sigh a sad farewell he took,
    Lumpaty, lumpaty, lump.
And all in despair he leapt into the brook,
    Flumpaty, flumpaty, flump.
His courage it cool'd, he found himself fool'd,
    Trumpaty, trumpaty, trump.
He swam to the shore and saw Dolly no more,
    Rumpaty, rumpaty, rump.

And then she recall'd and recall'd him again,
    Humpaty, humpaty, hump.
But he like a madman ran over the plain,
    Stumpaty, stumpaty, stump.
Determin'd to find a damsel more kind,
    Plumpaty, plumpaty, plump.
While Dolly's afraid she shall die an old maid,
    Mumpaty, mumpaty, mump.

JUSTIFICATION FOR LOVING

Saw you the nymph whom I adore ?
Saw you the goddess of my heart ?
And can you bid me love no more ?
And can you think I feel no smart ?

So many charms around her shine
Who can the sweet temptation fly ?
Spite of her scorn she's so divine
That I must love her though I die.

IN PRAISE OF LOVE

Love's a gentle, gen'rous passion,
    Source of all sublime delight,
When with mutual inclination
    Two fond hearts in one unite.

What are titles, pomp or riches,
    If compar'd with true content ?
That false joy which now bewitches
    When obtain'd, we may repent.

Lawless passions bring vexation,
    But a chaste and constant love
Is a glorious emulation
    Of the blissful state above.

LOVE ECSTATICK

A Song

To be gazing on those charms,
To be folded in those arms,
To unite my lips with those
Whence eternal sweetness flows ;
To be lov'd by one so fair
Is to be blest beyond compare.

On that bosom to recline,
While that hand is lock'd in mine ;
In those eyes myself to view,
Gazing still and still on you.
To be lov'd by one so fair
Is to be blest beyond compare.

LOVE'S A RIDDLE

A Song

The flame of love assuages
When once it is reveal'd ;
But faster still it rages
The more it is conceal'd.

Consenting makes it colder ;
When met it will retreat ;
Repulses make it bolder,
And dangers make it sweet.

A SONG

When Myrrha views me with disdain
My blood congeals, and ev'ry vein
With anguish shrinks, while wretched I
Beneath the mighty torment die.

But when the kind, consenting maid,
With eyes relenting, arms display'd,
Meeting, sooths me to her breast,
I glow, I burn, and am possest
Of joy too great to be express'd.

A SONG

A heart that's bleeding
With deep despair,
Is ne'er succeeding
Amongst the fair.

They hate imploring,
And courtship fly ;
Each swain adoring
Is sure to die.

HAPPY MYRTILLO

On a grassy pillow
The youthful Myrtillo
Transported was laid ;
In his arms a creature
Whose every feature
For conquest was made.

To his side he clasp'd her,
And fondly grasp'd her,
While she cry'd, Oh dear,
Oh dear Myrtillo,
Had I known your will, Oh,
I'd never come here.

Streams gently flowing,
And zephyrs blowing,
Ambrosial breeze ;
A swain admiring,
And all conspiring
The charmer to please :
The dear nymph complying,
No more denying
A silent grove.
Oh blest Myrtillo !
You may if you will, Oh,
Be happy as Jove.

Now the devill's in it
If such a minute
The shepherd would lose ;
No, no, no, Myrtillo
Has better skill, Oh
His moments to chuse ;
The delightful treasure
Of love and pleasure
He boldly seiz'd,
And like Myrtillo,
He had his fill, Oh,
Of what he pleas'd.

THE RIVAL LAP-DOG

Corinna, pray tell me
Why thus you repell me,
When humbly I sue for a kiss ;
While Dony at pleasure
May kiss without measure,
And surfeit himself with the bliss ?

How hard's my misfortune,
That I must importune
For what I must still be deny'd ;
While the rapturous duty
I owe to your beauty
Must be by a lap-dog supplied.

SONG IN *BRITANNIA*

Beauteous charmer, pride of nature,
Idol, goddess of my heart ;
Soul of sweetness, heaven-born creature,
Ease a tender lover's smart.
How I dote, adore, and languish
Witness all the gods above ;
Nothing can assuage my anguish
But a smile from her I love.

Ev'ry step inspires devotion,
Ev'ry look displays a grace ;
So majestick is your motion,
So angelick is your face ;
If there's pleasure in beholding
Such a boundless blaze of charms,
Oh, the rapture of enfolding
So much beauty in my arms !

AN EPITHALAMIUM

This is the day sacred to mirth and joy,
In which the happy, happy pair were join'd ;
Let boundless pleasure ev'ry soul employ ;
The swain is blest, the lovely nymph is coy.

A TOAST

Pass the glass around with pleasure,
'Tis the bride and bridegroom's health.
Send 'em blessing without measure,
Honour, peace, long life and wealth.

THE IMPATIENT LOVER

If there's transporting pleasure
    In gazing on your charms,
'Twere bliss beyond all measure
    To die within your arms.

Then, charmer, be not cruel,
    But give, O, give me ease.
Disdain is but the fuel
    That makes my flame increase.

THE INTREPID LOVER

No diamonds are so bright,
So alluring to the sight,
As the eyes of the nymph I admire.
I adore her cherry cheeks,
And she charms me when she speaks,
And her touch sets me all on fire.

I can no longer bear,
But I must my love declare ;
I'm resolved her intentions to know.
But if she proves too stout,
And makes too much rout,
To the devil she may go.

THE INCREDULOUS

Is there a wretch so stupid,
  So void of manly fire,
To be a slave to Cupid,
  And languish with desire ?

No ; surely human nature
  Its dictates must forget,
When to the weaker creature
  The nobler does submit.

THE EXPOSTULATION

Turn, turn away, mine eyes,
Make not a sacrifice
Of my poor Heart.
Tho' beyond measure
You share the pleasure,
That feels the smart.

THE INFERENCE

If it be true, as wise men say,
That women by contraries move,
It will be much the better way
For men to hate, that they may love.

For sighing and pining,
And canting and whining,
Are follies that blow up their pride ;
But if they once tack you,
They certainly back you,
And then to the D——l they'll ride.

LOVE WITHOUT ALLAY

Gazing on my idol-treasure,
All my soul is lost in joy ;
She affords eternal pleasure,
And can never, never cloy.

Ev'ry motion, ev'ry feature
Shines with such peculiar grace ;
Never, sure, was human creature
Blest with such an angel's face.

THE QUEEN OF HEARTS

A Song

Lovely ruler of my heart,
Queen of all and ev'ry part !
Object of my soul's desire,
For whose sake I could expire.

Witness ! all the gods above
That I only live to love ;
That I love but you alone,
Let me then my passion own.

Queen of my Heart, and idol of my soul,
I bless the pow'r that does each sense controul ;
So mild, so gentle is your reign,
I gladly wear the pleasing chain ;
Such pride I take your slave to be,
I would not, if I could, be free.

ON PARTHENISSA'S ABSENCE

Ye shady glooms, in vain you strive
Your verdant beauties to display ;
They rather pain than pleasure give
While Parthenissa is away.

But when the nymph returns again,
To bless these woods and Damon's arms,
Then I shall feel no lovesick pain,
And you'll possess your wonted charms.

A SONG

Wanton Cupids, cease to hover
Thus around the smiling fair;
You exclude a faithful lover,
With your too officious care.

Ye little loves, away, begone
To some remote and silent grove,
And leave Alexis here alone.
To tell his humble tale of love.

THE PRESUMPTUOUS LOVER

See, see, my Seraphina comes,
  Adorn'd with ev'ry grace.
Look, gods, from your celestial domes,
  And view her charming face.

Then search, and see if you can find
  In all your sacred groves,
Or nymph, or goddess, so divine
  As she whom Strephon loves.

THE ENCOURAGEMENT

Ah ! Silly, bashful, tim'rous Swain,
In love you're but a dunce.
No longer languish and complain,
But speak your mind at once.
She'll miff and she'll tiff,
And she'll seem to deny.
But sure as she pouts,
Flings, flounces and flouts,
So surely she'll comply.

How much, alas, is he perplex'd
Who's in a woman's power !
He's ever tortur'd, ever vext,
And ne'er at Peace an hour.
He's frolick, he's stupid, he's merry, he's sad,
One moment she'll please,
And another she'll teaze,
And make the poor soul stark mad.

THE QUEEN OF SPADES

Fairest of jades, thou art so smart
Thine eyes like spades dig out my heart.
Thou shalt be Queen of all the pack,
Let me but be thy darling Jack.

THE SUPPLICATION

Divinest fair,
O, ease my care,
And kindly cheer your dying swain ;
No longer fly,
No more deny,
But give me love for love again.

Love's powerful dart
Has pierc'd my heart,
Shot from your irresistless charms ;
Nor can I rest
Until I'm blest,
Encircl'd in your snowy arms.

THE LOVER'S COMPLAINT

If love's a folly, what am I,
Who love beyond expression ?
If 'tis a crime to be in love,
How great is my transgression !

Then cruel charmer, O ! be kind,
And pass my final sentence,
For I am weary of my chains,
And languish for repentance.

THE TELL-TALE

Blab not what you ought to smother ;
Honour's laws should sacred be.
Boasting favours from another
Ne'er will favours gain with me.
But, inspir'd with indignation,
Sooner I'd lead apes in hell
E'er I'd trust my reputation
With such fools that kiss and tell.

He who finds a hidden treasure
Never should the same reveal ;
Him whom beauty crowns with pleasure,
Cautious, should his joy conceal.
Him with whom my heart I'll venture
Shall my fame from censure save :
One where truth and prudence centre,
And as secret as the grave.

THE REVEILLE,

OR

A MORNING CALL TO THE BRIDE AND BRIDEGROOM

See, the morning gives you warning
To suspend your dear delight !
Rise to bless us and caress us,
Cupid bids you quit the fight.

CEPHALUS

In vain, alas, your charms invade
A heart that is another's due;
Were she I love by me betray'd,
That falsehood would not merit you.

To make my wavering heart your prize,
In vain your soft'ning art allures;
While Procris by my falsehood dies
I never, never, can be yours.

PROCRIS

Go, gentle sighs, pursue the wind,
Pass o'er the mountain, vale, and Grove
Till wand'ring Cephalus you find,
And echo to his ears my love.

Alarm his heart with all my fears,
Ah, tell him, tell him how I mourn;
A thousand frights, a thousand fears
Surround me till his dear return.

Go, gentle sighs, pursue the wind,
Pass o'er the mountain, vale and grove,
Till wand'ring Cephalus you find,
And echo to his ear my love.

THE PRECAUTION

(*Taken from a French Author*)

O nymph divinely charming,
Take heed thou art not charm'd ;
Be still all hearts alarming,
But never be alarm'd.

Love is a fatal anguish,
'Tis youth and beauty's bane ;
Let all men for you languish,
But ne'er regard their pain.

THE LOVER'S TRIUMPH

Ye beauteous nymphs and jovial swains,
Who worship at Cytherea's shrine,
With joyful echoes fill the plains,
For now the fair Olinda's mine.

Ye chirping birds, convey your notes
Through all the regions of the air ;
And stretch your little warbling throats
To tell she's kind, as well as fair.

A RECIPE FOR LOVE

Would you gain a woman's hate,
  Be a constant lover :
Would you woman's love create,
  Be a faithless rover.

The fond adorer they despise,
  And keep him in subjection ;
But he that woos with oaths and lies
  Is sure to gain affection.

ADVICE TO A FRIEND IN LOVE

Prithee, Billy,
Ben't so silly
Thus to waste thy days in grief ;
You say Betty
Will not let you,
But can sorrow give relief ?

Leave repining,
Cease your whining,
Pox on torment, grief and woe ;
If she's tender
She'll surrender,
If she's tough—e'en let her go.

LOVE AND JEALOUSY

A Sonnet

Tho' cruel you seem to my pain,
And hate me because I am true,
Yet, Phyllis, you love a false swain,
Who has other nymphs in his view :
Enjoyment's a trifle to him,
To me what a heav'n would it be.
To him but a woman you seem,
But, Ah ! you're an angel to me.

Those lips which he touches in haste,
To them I for ever could grow ;
Still clinging around that dear waist
Which he spans as beside him you go.
That hand, like a lilly so white,
Which over his shoulder you lay,
My bosom could warm it all night,
My lips they could press it all day.

Were I like a monarch to reign,
Were graces my subjects to be,
I'd leave them and fly to the plain,
To dwell in a cottage with thee.
But if I must feel your disdain,
If tears cannot cruelty drown,
Oh, let me not live in this pain !
But give me my death in a frown.

THE LANGUISHING LOVER

I sigh, I languish,
Yet I hide my anguish,
Lest I offend my charming fair ;
Should I reveal it
And she not heal it
My life must end in deep despair.

On fatal passion,
Fond inclination,
To love where I'm forbid to tell.
Tho' I conceal it,
My eyes reveal it,
My inmost soul she knows too well.

LOVE FOR LOVE'S SAKE

A Sonnet

I'll range around the shady bowers,
And gather all the sweetest flowers ;
I'll strip the garden and the grave
To make a garland for my love.

When in the sultry heat of day
My thirsty nymph does panting lay,
I'll hasten to the river's brink,
And drain the floods, but she shall drink.

At night, to rest her weary head,
I'll make my love a grassy bed ;
And with green boughs I'll form a shade,
That nothing may her rest invade.

And while dissolved in sleep she lies
Myself shall never close these eyes,
But, gazing still with fond delight,
I'll watch my charmer all the night.

And then, as soon as cheerful day
Dispels the darksome shades away,
Forth to the forest I'll repair,
To seek provision for my fair.

Thus will I spend the day and night,
Still mixing labour with delight,
Regarding nothing I endure,
So I can ease for her procure.

But if the nymph whom thus I love,
To her fond swain should faithless prove,
I'll seek some dismal, distant shore,
And never think of woman more.

THE INDIFFERENT LOVER

A Song

Should the nymph I love disdain me,
    And strive to give despair,
All her arts shall never pain me,
    For I'll seek a kinder fair.

Some think it mighty treasure
    A stubborn heart to gain ;
But theirs be all the pleasure,
    For 'tis not worth the pain.

THE WOMAN HATER

What's a woman but a name,
A pretty, empty, gaudy frame ;
Full of nonsense, full of pride,
Full of talk, and naught beside ?

Beauteous as angel's is her face,
She moves with more than human grace,
But who can prove, or who can find,
One single beauty in her mind ?

THE MAN HATER

What's man but a perfidious creature,
Of an inconstant, fickle nature,
Deceitful, and conceited too,
Boasting more than he can do ?

Beware, ye heedless nymphs, beware,
For men will lye, and fawn and swear ;
But when they once have gain'd the prize,
Good heav'ns ! how they will tyrannize !

THE FRIENDLY ADVISER

Trust not man, for he'll deceive you,
Treach'ry is his sole intent ;
First he'll court you, then he'll leave you,
Poor deluded to lament.
Listen to a kind adviser ;
Men pursue but to perplex ;
Would you happy be, grow wiser,
And avoid the faithless sex.

Form'd by nature to undo us,
They escape our utmost heed ;
Oh, how humble when they woo us,
Oh, how vain when they succeed !
So the bird, when once deluded
By the artful fowler's snare,
Mourns out life in cage secluded.
Virgins, then in time beware.

THE CONTRAST

Woman's an angelic creature
When with virtue she is crown'd ;
She's the masterpiece of nature,
Ev'ry joy in her is found.
When afflictions they o'ertake you
Yet a kind and constant mate ;
In distress will ne'er forsake you,
Struggling thro' the storms of fate.

But a false, deceitful harlot,
Who from in'trest sake is kind,
Fond alike of ev'ry varlet,
And inconstant as the wind.
Jilts you till she's quite undone you,
Then your error's found too late.
When she's fleec'd you, then she'll shun you,
Laughing, while you curse your fate.

AURORA

Oh ! silly swain, by love undone,
Was ever fair yet fair for one,
Or e'er by one for life caress'd ?
When rovers range for new delight,
The change with changing we requite,
And second thoughts are always best.

LOVE À LA MODE

Love's a fever of the mind,
'Tis a grief that none can cure
Till the nymph you love prove kind :
She can give you ease again,
She can best remove the pain
Which you for her endure.

Be not ever, then, repining,
Sighing, denying, canting, whining ;
Spend not time in vain pursuing ;
If she does not love you—make her ;
If she loves you—then forsake her ;
'Tis the modish way of wooing.

INJUR'D LOVE, OR THE MENACE

A Song

False, ungrateful traitor !
To wrong poor Celia so,
And leave so sweet a creature
To misery and woe.

Think not the gods forget you
They but retard your fate ;
When Celia finds their pity,
Then shalt thou feel their hate

THE DISCOURAGEMENT

Cease your addressing,
Your arts are in vain ;
You sue for a blessing
You ne'er will obtain.

The nymph you're pursuing
Is fatal as fair ;
You court but your ruin ;
Then, Strephon, beware.

THE MAID'S PETITION

Cruel creature, can you leave me.
Can you then ungrateful prove ?
Did you court me to deceive me,
And to slight my constant love ?

False, ungrateful, thus to woo me,
Thus to make my heart a prize ;
First to ruin and undo me,
Then to scorn and tyrannize.

Shall I send to Heaven my prayer ?
Shall I all my wrongs relate ?
Shall I curse the dear betrayer ?
No, alas ! it is too late.

Cupid, pity my condition,
Pierce the unrelenting swain.
Hear a tender maid's petition,
And restore my love again.

MOLLY'S COMPLAINT

In some dreary desert I'll hide me,
Regardless of what shall betide me ;
The herbage with food shall provide me,
And savages pity my moan.

I'll sleep at the foot of some mountain,
I'll drink of the chrystalline fountaine,
And while I'm my sorrows recounting,
Kind echo shall answer each groan.

The swain I adore has undone me,
He woo'd me untill he had won me,
He courted me sure but to shun me,
And now from his arms am I thrown.

My musick is turn'd to lamenting,
My triumphs to tears and repenting,
From all humane creatures absenting,
I wander dejected alone.

Come, death, from distraction relieve me,
Cold earth to thy bosom receive me,
Come thou who so basely couldst leave me,
And shed one kind tear on my stone.

NOAH'S DOVE

Pastora by some matchless art
First made me feel the lover's pain ;
But soon my disappointed heart,
Like Noah's dove, return'd again.

Another resting place is sought,
Entic'd by Phoebe's sprightly mien ;
And, like the wand'ring bird, it brought
A certain signal where't had been.

But soon as Emma bless'd my sight
With all the charms in virtue's store ;
Like that same dove it took its flight,
And finding rest, return'd no more.

THE LOVER'S COMPLAINT

Ah, cruel fair,
Can you leave me to despair ?
Or see my woe,
And yet no pity show ?
Oh, hear your swain,
Relieve my pain,
Or death will soon remove
The wretch you cannot love !

Must all those charms
Fill my happy rival's arms ?
Must I repine,
Yet never see you mine ?

O hapless fate !
O causeless hate !
Yet, spite of your disdain,
I still embrace my chain.

May you be blest,
And of all you wish possesst ;
While in some cave
Poor I distracted rave ;
Woods, rocks and stones
Shall hear my groans,
And greater pity show
Than you that caus'd my woe.

THE TANTALIZING LOVER

Cruel charmer, tell me why
You'll not let me live or die ?
First your smiles they give me joy,
Then your frowns my hopes destroy.
When you see my raging pain,
Out of sport you smile again.

Thus with a tyrannic art
You torment my bleeding heart,
Taking pleasure in my grief,
Yet affording no relief.
O, pronounce my doom outright,
And in pity kill me quite !

A MAD SONG

I go to the Elysian shades
Where sorrow ne'er shall wound me ;
Where nothing shall my rest invade,
But joy shall still surround me.
I fly from Celia's cold disdain,
From her disdain I fly ;
She is the cause of all my pain,
For her alone I die.
Her eyes are brighter than the mid-day sun,
When he but half his radiant course has run,
When his meridian glories gaily shine,
And gild all nature with a warmth divine.
See yonder river's flowing tide,
Which now so full appears,
Those streams that do so sweetly glide
Are nothing but my tears.
There have I wept till I could weep no more,
And curst mine eyes when they have shed their store ;
Then, like the clouds that rob the azure main,
I've drain'd the flood to weep it back again.
          Pity my pains,
          Ye gentle swains.
     Cover me with ice and snow,
I scorch, I burn, I flame, I glow ;
          Furies tear me,
          Quickly bear me
To the dismal shades below,
          Where yelling and howling,
          And grumbling and growling,
Strike our ears with horrid woe.
          Hissing snakes,
          Fiery lakes,
Were a pleasure and a cure ;

Not all the hills
Where Pluto dwells
Can give such pains as I endure.
　　To some peaceful plain convey me,
　　Fan me with ambrosial breeze !
　　Let me die, and so have ease !

SECOND MAD SONG

Gods ! I can never this endure,
Death alone must be my cure.
I groan, I sink beneath the weight
Of Celia's cruel, causeless hate.
　　Why was she made so fair ?
　　Why are her eyes so bright ?
　　They kill me with despair,
　　And yet attract my sight.
In her eyes a thousand stars
　　Centre their brightness ;
In her face a thousand charms
　　Display their sweetness.
But she is proud as Juno's haughty self ;
Ah ! 'tis a proud, disdainful, charming elf !
　　Who e'er becomes a victim to her eyes,
　　She makes his bleeding heart a sacrifice.
　　While on a downy bed
Of mossy grass I lay my lovesick head,
　　And seek for soft repose,
Her angel form around me flies,
Awakes my soul, forbids mine eyes
　　Their falling lids to close.
　　Then to the limpid stream
　　With eager haste I fly,

234

And midst the waters plunge,
    With sure intent I die,
When Lo ! some wretch by evil gods design'd
To lengthen out the torments of mankind,
With cursed friendship drags me thence again,
And makes me live but to endure more pain.
    But I have found a way
    That shall her scorn repay ;
I'll leave this false, imaginary light,
And seek the dismal shades of night.
    With goblins and fairies
    I'll dance the canaries,
And demons all round in a ring ;
    With witches I'll fly
    Beneath the cold sky,
And with the screech-owl will I sing.
    My love, alas !
    Is dead and gone,
    She's dead and gone to me :
And now my senses they are flown,
    I have my liberty.

THE CURE OF LOVE

My friends could give me no relief;
No balm could reach my inward grief;
Nothing could ease my tortur'd mind,
Because Lucinda was unkind.

Oft on a flow'ry bank I lay,
And weeping spent the tedious day;
As oft by silver streams I stood,
And with my tears increas'd the flood.

On cypress banks I oft engrav'd
Her name, who had my soul enslav'd,
And oft, to all the echoes round
I would repeat the pleasing sound.

To food and rest a stranger grown,
My body wasted to the bone;
Thought I—this cannot long endure,
It would be best to seek a cure.

I call'd my friends, who brought me wine
Of sparkling colour, taste divine!
Then to the brim we charg'd our glasses,
And drank adieu to all coy lasses.

Scarce had we pass'd six bumpers round
When lo, my wond'rous power I found;
My reason had assum'd its throne,
And all the fumes of love were gone!

Now I, who was so sad of late,
Began to laugh, and sing, and prate;
My cheeks, which had been pale before,
A flush of ruby brightness wore.

My eyes they sparkled with delight,
My mind was gay, my heart was light ;
With songs of joy I fill'd the place,
And pleasure triumph'd in my face.

Now could I name the cruel fair
Without or anguish, or despair ;
Could tell her ev'ry fault aloud,
Nay, call her jilt, coquette, and proud.

And now Lucinda I despise,
Wine, glorious wine alone I prize ;
Wine, that can all our griefs remove,
And cure the raging pain of love.

A CURE FOR LOVE

Cupid no more shall give me grief,
Or anxious cares oppress my soul,
While generous Bacchus brings relief,
And drowns 'em in a flowing bowl.

Celia, thy scorn I now despise,
Thy boasted empires I disown :
This takes the brightness from thy eyes,
And makes it sparkle in my own.

THE CONFLICT BETWEEN LOVE AND WINE

Alone by a lonely willow
Poor Damon sighing lay.
The grass was his only pillow,
Alack, and well-a-day.

I came with my flask,
And I gave him a drink ;
Had it been a whole cask
He'd have drunk it I think.

He danc'd and he sung,
And he caper'd like mad,
And swore he'd have more
If more could be had.

But Celia, with charms surrounded,
Came tripping it o'er the plain ;
The shepherd afresh was wounded,
And all undone again.

He call'd her his goddess, she call'd him an ass ;
I ply'd him again with a cherishing glass ;
He laugh'd at her scorn, and her pow'r he defy'd,
And vow'd his dear bottle should alone be his bride.

SIMON SNUGG,

OR

THE SAFE ONE

To banish care when stocks were sinking,
Six jolly fellows got to drinking,
And wisely laid aside dull thinking.
While misers they with thirst were choking,
These merry souls were drinking, smoking,
Laughing, quaffing, singing, joking,
And bravely drank six flasks apiece,
While worldlings fretted in their grease.
Ever scolding, never holding,
Ever teasing, never ceasing,
Is my sweet, dear, precious spouse ;
Ever merry, ever airy,
Ever smiling, care beguiling,
Still am I when I carouse.

Shall I lose the comfort of my life ?
Shall I leave my bottle for my wife ?
Let her scold, I do not fear it ;
I'll get where I shall not hear it,
For I'll drown myself in claret.

CATO'S ADVICE

Interponere tuis interdum gaudia curis,
Ut possis animo quemvis sufferre laborem.

What Cato advises
Most certainly wise is,
Not always to labour, but sometimes to play ;
To mingle sweet pleasure
With search after treasure,
Indulging at night for the toils of the day.

And while the dull miser
Esteems himself wiser
His bags to increase, he his youth will decay ;
Our souls we enlighten,
Our fancies we brighten,
And pass the long evening in pleasure away.

All cheerful and hearty,
We set aside party,
With some tender fair each bright bumper is
  crown'd ;
Thus Bacchus invites us,
Thus Venus delights us,
While care in an ocean of claret is drown'd.

See, here's our physician,[1]
We know no ambition,
For where there's good wine and good company
  found,
Thus happy together,
In spite of all weather
'Tis sunshine and summer with us the year round.

---

[1] Pointing to the bottle.

A BACCHANALIAN SONG

Come, all ye jolly bacchanals,
Who love to tope good wine,
Let us offer up a hogshead
Unto our master's shrine.
Then let us drink, and never shrink,
For I'll tell you the reason why.
'Tis a great sin to leave a house
Till we've drunk the cellar dry.

In times of old I was a fool,
I drank the water clear ;
But Bacchus took me from that rule,
He thought 'twas too severe.
He fill'd a goblet to the brim,
And bade me take a sup ;
And had it been a gallon-pot,
By Jove ! I'd toss'd it up.

And ever since that happy time
Good wine has been my cheer.
Now nothing puts me in a swoon
But water, or small beer.
Then let us tope a bout, my boys,
And never flinch nor fly,
But fill our skins with generous wine,
And drain the bottles dry.

A BACCHANALIAN RANT

In the Bombast Strain

Bacchus must now his pow'r resign,
I am the only god of wine :
It is not fit the wretch should be
In competition set with me,
Who can drink ten times more than he.

Make a new world, ye pow'rs divine !
Stock'd with nothing else but wine :
Let wine its only product be,
Let wine be earth, and air, and sea,
And let that wine be—all for me.

Let other mortals vainly wear
A tedious life in anxious care ;
Let the ambitious toil and think ;
Let states or empires swim or sink ;
My sole ambition is to *drink*.

A BACCHANALIAN SCENE

Supposed to be acted at a Tavern by a Set of
True-Topers. In the Brobdignan Measure

FIRST TOPER :   Pray pull the ribbon, sir.
    (*Second Toper rings and calls*)
    Here, drawer !
    (*Enter Drawer*)
    Gentlemen, d'ye call ?

THIRD TOPER :   We've rang this half-hour, bring more wine ; d'ye mean to parch us all ?

DRAWER :   Why, gentleman, the wine you seal'd is drunk out ev'ry Flask.

FOURTH TOPER :   Then down into the cellar, boys, and there let's broach a cask :
Thou to each mouth shall pierce a hole, while we kneel down and suck ;
O, what a consort there will be, of Gluck, Gluck, Gluck, Gluck, Gluck.

Scene changes to the wine cellar, where they all make
a low reverence to a hogshead of claret

FIRST TOPER :   Lovely wet-nurse ! dear foster mother of the tippling race !
The goodness of thy milk is seen in ev'ry ruby face.

SECOND TOPER : How many sad and mournful hearts
      hast thou reviv'd and chear'd ?
    How many glorious, precious babes,
      dear nursey, hast thou rear'd ?

THIRD TOPER : 'Tis time she had a little ease ; poor
    soul ! she is too full :
    The draughts come in ; see how she
      swells ! Come, pull away boys,
      pull !
    (*They all kneel down and suck*)

FOURTH TOPER : Oh, glorious milk ! how sweet, how
    pure ! Let sneakers take their
    flask,
    I'll never touch a bottle more while
    I can suck a cask.

CHORUS

O, glorious milk, how sweet, how pure ! Let sneakers
    take their flask,
I'll never touch a bottle more while I can suck a cask.

THE SPUNGER

Toby Swill
Has ne'er his fill,
Tho' he drinks from night to day ;
But soon as e'er
The reck'ning's call'd.
Then Toby sneaks away.

Toby laughs,
And puns, and quaffs,
Until a bill is call'd ;
That strikes him dumb,
He's then hum-drum,
And all his mirth is pall'd.

Pay but his shot,
'Tis all forgot,
And he again is gay ;
He'll stand the rub
Of a whole club,
To drink, and not to pay.

THE TOPER'S TOAST

Here's to thee, my boy,
My darling, my joy,
For a toper I love as my life ;
Who ne'er baulks his glass,
Nor cries like an ass
To go home to his children and wife.

But heartily quaffs,
Sings, eats, dies, and laughs,
All the night he looks jovial and gay ;
When morning appears,
Then homeward he steers,
To snore out the rest of the day.

He feels not the cares,
The griefs nor the fears
That the sober too often attend ;
Nor knows he a loss,
Disturbance or cross,
Save the want of his bottle and friend.

HARRY CAREY'S REPLY TO THE LIBELLING GENTRY WHO ARE ANGRY AT HIS WELFARE

Quod me Roma legit, rumpitur invidia,
Rumpitur invidia, quod sum jucundus amicis,
Rumpitur invidia, quod amamur, quodque probamur ;
Rumpatur, quisquis rumpitur invidia.
Mart., Lib. IX.

With an honest old friend and a merry old song,
And a flask of old port let me sit the night long,
And laugh at the malice of those who repine
That they must swig porter, while I can drank wine.

I envy no mortal tho' ever so great,
Nor scorn I a man for his lowly estate :
But what I abhor and esteem as a curse
Is poorness in spirit, not poorness in purse.

Then dare to be generous, dauntless, and gay,
Let's merrily pass life's remainder away :
Upheld by our friends we our foes may despise,
For the more we are envied, the higher we rise.

A DRINKING SONG

Sons of Bacchus, let's be gay,
Nimbly move the cheerful glass ;
Life is short and glides away,
Let it then in pleasure pass.
Phoebus now may hide his light,
Silver Cynthia cease to shine ;
Bacchus' rays are far more bright,
Sparkling from the generous wine.

When the nymph is coy and cold,
And puts on a scornful air,
Bacchus makes the lover bold ;
Courage ever gains the fair.
While the fool who wastes his time
Trifling o'er insipid tea,
Ne'er can aim at things sublime,
Till he freely drinks like me.

THE TOAST

Fill, Fill, Fill a brimming glass ;
Each man toast his favourite lass.
He that flinches is an ass,
Unworthy love or wine.

Bacchus crowns the flowing bowl,
Wine does all our cares controul,
Love exalts a human soul,
And makes it next divine.

O, I feel it cheer my heart ;
'Tis a sin so soon to start ;
Let us drink, before we part,
A health to thine and mine.

THE MERRY GREGORIANS[1]

Let poets and historians
Record the brave Gregorians
In long and lasting lays ;
With hearts and voices joining,
In gladsome songs combining,
Sing forth their deathless praise.

If innocent variety,
Content and sweet society
Can make us mortals blest ;
In social love united,
With harmony delighted
We emulate the best.

Our friendship and affinity
Surpasses consanguinity,
As gold surpasses ore ;
Success to ev'ry brother,
Let's stand by one another
Till time shall be no more.

THE AUTHOR'S QUIETUS

Address'd to his Dear Friend, Jemmy Worsdale[1]

This itch of scribbling has no end, no ease,
Damn'd if you fail, and envy'd if you please ;
Uncertain pleasure for most certain pain :
Well, Solomon says right, All things are vain ;
'Tis better that a man should eat and drink.
Here !—Take away this ugly pen and ink !
Come, James !—let's have a bottle and a bit ;
There's something solid in that kind of wit.

NOTES

AN EPILOGUE TO THE SAME ENTERTAINMENT

[1] *Great Anna will a lasting Peace obtain*—An obvious reference to the Treaty of Utrecht (1713). For the importance of this, see Introduction. p. 14.

PROLOGUE TO " THE RIVAL QUEENS "

[1] A play by Colley Cibber, first acted at the Haymarket Theatre on June 29, 1710.

[2] Perhaps an ironical gibe at the pompous heroic couplet measures put into the mouths of kings and heroes in contemporary tragedy.
Cf. Prologue to *Chrononhotonthologos* (1734):—
Tonight our comick Muse the Buskin wears,
And gives herself no small romantick airs,
Struts in Heroicks, and in pompous Verse
Does the minutest Incident rehearse.

EPILOGUE SPOKEN BY MR. CIBBER, JUNR., 1729

This poem is not included in any of Carey's volumes, but it is printed on page 86 of Joseph Yarrow's *Choice Collection of Poetry* (1738), where the author is given as " Mr. Carey."
Mr. Cibber, Junr., of course, is Theophilus Cibber, the actor son of Colley Cibber.

SUNG BY MRS. CLIVE IN " COLUMBINE COURTEZAN "

[1] A pantomime, performed at Drury Lane 2/2/1734.

THE INTRIGUE

[1] An Interlude by Colley Cibber, acted at Drury Lane 6/10/1711. In 1729 Carey introduced this song into the revised Ballad-Opera version of his own *Contrivances*.

EPILOGUE INTENDED FOR MR. CIBBER'S NEW PASTORAL CALL'D " LOVE IN A RIDDLE "

[1] Acted at Drury Lane 7/1/1729.

[2] *Cuzzoni.* Francesca Cuzzoni (1700–1770), an Italian opera singer, very popular in England at this time. Her first appearance in London was on January 12, 1722, as Teofane in Handel's *Otho*.

EPILOGUE TO " THE PURITAN "

[1] A Pseudo-Shakespearean Comedy, published in quarto, 1607. The initials W. S. appeared on the title page as those of the author, and the play was included in the third folio, but it is certainly not by Shakespeare.

THE HAPPY NUPTIALS

[1] This poem is printed in the *Gentleman's Magazine* for November, 1733. It was written in honour of the coming marriage of the Princess Anne to the Prince of Orange.

THE PRINCE OF ORANGE'S MARCH

[1] *Britannia*—an entertainment given at Goodman's Fields Theatre 11/2/1734 in honour of the same occasion.

THE WEDDING DAY

[1] *Master Osborne.* Richard Osborne was a pupil of Carey's, and also acted in the capacity of an amanuensis to him. He died in 1737 at the early age of nineteen. In the preface to the first edition of *The Musical Century* Carey pays a tribute to his ability as a musician, while the same volume contains a poem lamenting his death. (See page 192 of the present work).

[2] *The Happy Nuptials.* A Musical Entertainment given at Goodman's Fields Theatre, 12/11/1733.

A LOYAL SONG SUNG AT THE THEATRES

[1] Carey's authorship of this song has long been in dispute. The first appearance of the complete piece, as here given, was in the *Gentleman's Magazine* for October, 1745, where both the words and the music were printed, but no name of the author was given. The tune and two

stanzas had previously appeared in a collection, *Thesaurus Musicus* (c. 1740), but again no author's name is given, though Carey is mentioned as one of the principal contributors to the volume. One piece only bears his name. His claim to authorship was first put forward in 1795 by his son, George Savile Carey, who alleged that J. C. Smith, a friend and collaborator of the elder Carey had declared him to be the author. This claim was supported by Dr. Harrington, of Bath, and at about the same time a correspondent of *The Gentleman's Magazine* vouched that he had first heard the song at a tavern in Cornhill in 1740, when it was sung by Carey in celebration of the victory of Admiral Vernon over the Spaniards at Portobello. Much evidence, however, has been put forward to refute Carey's claim. For a full discussion of the question the reader is referred to *God Save the King*, by R. Clark (1822) and *The National Anthem*, by W. H. Cummings (1902). The present editor would venture to suggest that it was composed by Carey in the heat of an anti-Spanish fervour in 1739, sung by him in 1740, printed in *Thesaurus Musicus* soon after, and then with the Jacobite rebellion of 1745, was seized on by the people and used as " a loyal song," since which time it has become popular.

A BALLAD ON THE TIMES

[1] *Folks have a Care of the Steeple*. Evidently a political slogan, used to signify High Church tyranny.

THE METHODIST PARSON

[1] *Mother Map*. A quack-physician of Epsom. She is the subject of many contemporary skits and satires.

A HUE AND CRY AFTER M—K

[1] The authorship of this piece is in doubt. It appears amongst none of Carey's poems, but was published as a broadside sheet in 1726. The catalogue of the British Museum assigns it to Thomas Gordon, a political and religious writer, but no name is attached to the poem other than " by the author of *Namby-Pamby*." Confusion may have arisen from the fact that in the previous year *Namby-Pamby* had been wrongly printed as by " Captain Gordon, author of the *Humourist*."

253

A SATIRE ON THE LUXURY AND EFFEMINACY OF THE AGE

[1] The waxwork show, kept by Mrs. Salmon, near St. Dunstan's Church in Fleet Street, was popular until well past the middle of the century.

[2] *Cuzzoni.* An Italian opera singer. See note to *The Epilogue to Love in a Riddle,* above.

[3] *Senesino.* Francesco Bernardi Senesino (1680–1750), a famous Italian Opera Singer and Sopranist. He came to London with Handel in 1720, but later quarrelled with him and, with several other Italian singers, seceded from the company to set up a rival opera in Lincoln's Inn Fields. At the Haymarket Theatre in 1731 he was receiving a salary of one thousand four hundred guineas. He returned to Italy in 1739, having amassed a fortune of well over fifteen thousand pounds.

[4] *Poor Robinson.* Anastasia Robinson (c. 1698–1755), an English singer eclipsed by the advent of Cuzzoni.

[5] *Bononcini.* Giovanni Battista Bononcini (or Buonincini), the most famous of a well-known Italian musical family. He came to London in 1720, and in association with Handel produced a number of operas.

[6] *Bernardi.*—Senesino.—See note 3, above.

[7] *Honest Dick.* Richard Leveridge (c. 1670–1758), a fellow musician of Carey, and author of the words and music of the well-known song *The Roast Beef of Old England.* He composed the music for an operatic version of *Macbeth* given at Drury Lane in 1702. He had a splendid voice, reputed to be the best in England, and for thirty years he sang in pantomimes and operatic pieces at Lincoln's Inn Fields and Covent Garden.

OF STAGE TYRANTS

For the origin of this poem, see Introduction, pp. 38.

[1] *When Booth, Wilks, Cibber rul'd the Stage.* On January 27, 1719, the Lord Chamberlain granted a license for the production of plays at Drury Lane Theatre to Barton Booth, John Wilks, and Colley Cibber. (See Public Record Office, Lord Chamberlain's Documents 5/156.) The Old Drury Lane Company broke up in 1731, soon after which Fleetwood acquired the rights.

[2] *Cibber, Terror of the Scribbling Crew.* Of the triumvirate at Drury Lane, Cibber was, according to all contemporary accounts, the most difficult to get on with, being curt, short tempered, frank, and often rather dictatorial to authors.

[3] *The Man of Taste.* A Comedy by James Miller, produced at Drury Lane 6/3/1735.

[4] *Vide* the Ballad of *Sally in Our Alley*, page 151.

THE BEAU'S LAMENTATION FOR THE LOSS OF FARRINELLI

[1] *Farrinelli.* Carlo Broschi, surnamed Farrinelli, a famous opera singer (castrato). He came from Italy to England in 1734, where he joined the rival opera company to Handel at Lincoln's Inn Fields. As a singer he earned instant popularity, and became a demi-god to the polite company of the town. On June 11, 1737 he went to Spain.

[2] All well-known actors who took part in many of Carey's own plays.

[3] The famous actress who had previously made a name for herself as Miss Raftor.

[4] Carey's burlesque opera, *The Dragon of Wantley*, produced at Covent Garden 26/10/1737. Margery = Margery Gubbins, the heroine ; Mauxy = Mauxalinda, a cast off mistress of the hero. Laguerre was an actor in the piece.

[5] *Heidegger.* John James Heidegger, manager of the Italian Opera at the Haymarket.

[6] *Strada.* Anna Strada del Po, an Italian soprano. She came to England with Handel in 1729, and remained loyal to him through his long dispute with the rival company. She finally departed the country as the result of a quarrel with Heidegger.

[7] Hickford was the proprietor of a room in the Haymarket, where musical pieces were frequently performed after 1739.

NAMBY-PAMBY

[1] A.... P...., Esq. Ambrose Phillips (see Introd., p. 36).

[2] *Andromache.* A reference to Phillips' play *The Distrest Mother* (Drury Lane 17/3/1712), the heroine of which is Andromache.

A NEW YEAR'S ODE.

[1] Colley Cibber was poet laureate from 1730 to 1757.

THE HAPPY BEGGARS

This poem is attributed to Carey by Moffat and Kidson in their *Minstrelsy of England* (1901). " His name," state the authors, " is inscribed in an old hand in ink, on one copy." The piece first appeared anonymously in Walsh's *Merry Musician* (1716), Vol. I. It was subsequently reprinted in several contemporary anthologies, but in none is the name of the author given.

THE MODERATOR BETWEEN THE FREEMASONS AND THE GORMOGONS

[1] *The Gormogons.* A society founded in the early eighteenth century in imitation of the Freemasons. Pope (*The Dunciad*, iv, 576) describes them as " A sort of lay brothers, slips from the root of the Freemasons."

SALLY SWEETBREAD

[1] *Fielding, Oates, Hall.* Mountebank actors and proprietors of theatrical booths at Bartholomew Fair.

[2] *Hippesley.* John Hippesley, dramatist, actor, and proprietor of a booth at Bartholomew Fair. He played the original part of Peachum in *The Beggar's Opera*.

[3] *Pinchbeck.* Christopher Pinchbeck (1670–1732), a maker of clocks and musical automata, which he exhibited at fairs.

[4] *Fawkes.* A well-known juggler. He was a companion and fellow exhibitor of Pinchbeck.

POLLY PEACHUM

[1] *Rolli.* Paulo Antonio Rolli, reputed to have been a baker and pastrycook by profession, came to England from Italy in 1718 and obtained an engagement as a singer upon the stage. He proved very popular, and was employed by managers to supply libretti to the Italian operas which were at that time being presented to the English public. He left the country in 1744.

[2] *Man's and White's.* Two well-known coffee-houses. Man's, the most fashionable house in London, was situated behind Charing Cross, near Scotland Yard. It was kept

by an Alexander Man, from whom it took its name, and was frequented by all the beaux. White's was a combined coffee-house and club, where many of the wits of the day gathered to discuss the latest scandal.

[3] " *The Beggar's Opera*," for which all the author's friends prophesied damnation, was a great success, supporting a run of sixty-two nights (not sixty-three as Genest says). Rich, the manager of Covent Garden, accepted the play when all others had rejected it, a stroke of foresight which a wag of the day commended by saying that it had made Gay rich, and Rich gay.

SALLY IN OUR ALLEY

[1] *Sally Salisbury*. A notorious character who led a debauched life amongst the gallants of the time. Her real name was Sarah Priddon, but she was always known as Sally Salisbury. Three works relating to her are still extant, viz. : *Memoirs of The Celebrated Sally Salisbury ; The Conversations of Sally Salisbury ;* and *Sally Salisbury's Letter to F. Rig*—all published in 1723.

[2] *Bedlam.* Bedlam (Bethlehem Hospital), was at this time situated in Moorfields, on the site now occupied by Liverpool Street Station. Until the year 1770 the London public could pay twopence to see the lunatics, and this asylum was considered one of the sights of London. Ned Ward, in chapter iii of *The London Spy* (1703), a veritable storehouse of information on life in the metropolis in the early years of the eighteenth century, gives a lengthy account of a visit to Bedlam.

A WHIMSICAL DIALOGUE BETWEEN THE AUTHOR AND HIS FAVOURITE MARE

[1] *Your brats and Will.* William Savile Carey, the poet's third son, born February 25, 1740.

[2] *My daughter Clive.* The poet's daughter, Catherine Clive Carey, born November 14, 1735.

ON THE DEATH OF THE LATE FAMOUS MR. ELFORD

[1] *Mr. Elford.* Richard Elford (d. Oct. 29, 1714), a lay vicar of St. Paul's and Westminster Abbey, was famous as a singer of sacred music in London.

[2] Elford was sworn a gentleman of the Chapel Royal on August 2, 1702.

THE STAGG AT BAY

[1] *Apollo and Daphne.* A pantomime by John Thurmond, performed at Drury Lane 11/2/1726.

THE DISTRESS'D FATHER.

[1] *His dear Daughter Rachel.* No record of the death of this child is to be found. The same poem again appears in, *A Choice Collection of Poetry* (1738) by Joseph Yarrow, page 18, as " by a gentleman whose misfortune it was to lose his only daughter by the small pox at five years of age."

EPITAPH INTENDED FOR MRS. SUSANNAH WORSDALE

[1] *Mrs. Susannah Worsdale.* The wife of James Worsdale, the author's friend. *Vide* page 250 and note on page 260.

THE CYPRESS GROVE

[1] *Olaus Westeinson Linnert.* A well-known musician, and one of Carey's teachers in his early years.

THE MUSE'S TEARS

[1] *Richard Osborne.* *Vide* note to page 77.

TO THE RIGHT HONOURABLE RICHARD, EARL OF BURLINGTON

This poem is the dedicatory epistle to the printed edition of Carey's opera *Teraminta* (1732).

TO THE RIGHT HONOURABLE CHARLES, VISCOUNT BRUCE

This poem forms the dedicatory epistle to the 1737 edition of *The Musical Century.*

TO MY STUDIOUS FRIEND, MR. JOHN FREDERICK LAMPE

[1] *Lampe.* A fellow musician of Carey's. He composed the music for Carey's opera *Teraminta*, and for his two burlesques, *The Dragon of Wantley*, and *Margery*, its sequel.

TO MR. OBADIAH SHUTTLEWORTH

[1] Obadiah Shuttleworth (1675–1734) was well known as the transcriber of Corelli's works. He was an expert violinist, and in 1724 became organist at the church of St. Michael, Cornhill.

TO THE MEMORY OF MR. GEORGE HAYDEN

[1] *George Hayden.* Organist of the Church of St. Mary Magdalene, Bermondsey.

TO MR. MATTHEW DUBOURG

[1] Matthew Dubourg (1703–1767) was well known as a violinist. Like Carey, he was a pupil of Geminiani.

TO MR. GALLIARD

[1] *Mr. Galliard.* A fellow musician and friend of Carey. According to George Savile Carey, it was on Galliard's authority that he claimed *God Save the King* as his father's composition.

TO MR. GEMINIANI

[1] Francesco Geminiani (1667–1762), violinist and composer. He was one of Carey's early teachers.

TO DR. PEPUSCH

[1] John Christopher Pepusch (1667–1752) was German by birth. He came to England about 1700, and was engaged in the orchestra at Drury Lane Theatre. In 1713 he was appointed musical director to the theatre in Lincoln's Inn Fields, which position he held for some years. He set several of the songs in *The Beggar's Opera.*

TO MR. THOMAS ROSEINGRAVE

[1] Thomas Roseingrave (1690–1766) came of a musical family, his father being Daniel Roseingrave, the organist of St. Patrick's and Christ Church, Dublin. In 1725 the son was appointed the first organist at St. George's, Hanover Square, which position he was forced to relinquish in 1737 owing to ill-health. He was one of Carey's early teachers, and composed many pieces for the organ and the harpsichord.

THE HAPPY MARRIAGE

[1] *Nathaniel Oldham.* A collector of natural and artificial curiosities. One of his principal acquisitions was " a choice collection of butterflies."

THE MERRY GREGORIANS

[1] *The Gregorians.* A society which flourished in London before 1738. Carey was a member. Its chief occupation was eating and drinking.

[1] *Jemmy Worsdale*. James Worsdale (1692–1767), a dabbler in all the arts and, according to Laetitia Pilkington (*The Memoirs of Laetitia Pilkington*), a person of very dissolute character. He attempted dramatic composition, poetry, music and painting, as well as acting. He seems to have been well versed in all the tricks and subterfuges of the underworld of letters of his day, and willingly became the tool of Pope in his attempt to defraud Curll in the matter of his correspondence. Many poems were printed under his name, but, states Mrs. Pilkington, " I can assure the world that Mr. Worsdale never wrote a line of poetry in his life," and later, " all the world knows that Mr. Pilkington and Harry Carey were his understrappers or subalterns in poetical stock-jobbery." He painted a portrait of Carey, engravings of which are still extant.

APPENDIX

JAMES RALPH came to England in 1724 in the company of Benjamin Franklin, and after struggling to earn a living as a hack writer and a schoolmaster finally became friendly with Fielding, in whose work Ralph's influence is plainly visible. (On this subject see a paper entitled " Fielding's Indebtedness to James Ralph," by Miss Helen S. Hughes, in *Modern Philology*, Vol. xx, 1922.) Carey seems also to have fallen under his influence. The year 1728 saw the publication of Ralph's volume of essays, *The Touchstone ; or Critical, Historical, Political, Philosophical and Theological Essays on the Reigning Diversions of the Town*, from which Carey took the hint for his burlesque opera, *The Dragon of Wantley*, performed in 1737, but probably written several years earlier. In the first essay of *The Touchstone* appears the following passage relative to Italian operas :

" I am sensible that their being performed in a foreign tongue disgusts many of my countrymen who (tho' no great Philhar-monicks), yet being true Britons and staunch Protestants, to show their love for their country and their zeal for their religion, are possessed against singing as well as praying in an unknown dialect."

There certainly seems an echo of this in the stanza,

" I hate this singing . . . .
. . . . . be singing Mass."
(Page 99 of the present text)

from *A Satire on the Luxury and Effeminacy of the Age*, a poem on the same subject publish only one year later than Ralph's work.

H